MW00534255

THIS PLAYBOOK BELONGS TO

_____

BLACK JOY *Play* BOOK

30 Days of Intentionally Reclaiming Your Delight

Tracey Michae'l Lewis-Giggetts

Ink & Willow

To all of us who are reclaiming our joy and getting free.

I've . . . learned that joy is an inside job. For a season, it might be okay to chase it. But at some point, we have to cultivate it on the inside so that no [person or] place . . . has the power to steal joy from us.

TRACEY MICHAE'L LEWIS-GIGGETTS,
Black Joy: Stories of Resistance, Resilience, and Restoration

CONTENTS

JOY IN THE TEARS

JOY IN THE LAUGHTER

JOY IN THE EVERY DAY

Introduction

TRUSTING THE SILENCE

In 2019, the only place where I felt well was my bed. If I stood for any length of time, I became dizzy. My limbs were a weight that made me feel as though I were walking through mud. Every muscle in my body would periodically tighten like a vice grip squeezing the life out of me. At least that's the way it felt. And the worst part of it? There wasn't a single doctor who could explain what was happening to me.

In hindsight, I understand that my body had simply had enough. It was done with all my running around. All the wear and tear. All the hustling and grinding I thought I needed to do to feel worthy and valuable and loved. It had collapsed under the weight of grief I'd yet to reckon with. So my body had decided to shut down, seemingly in protest.

I was left with nothing else but my bed and the silence.

Oh, the silence. That was probably the hardest thing to bear. I was used to the noise. I was comfortable with all the voices in my head pushing me to do more, more, more. The voices of all those parts of me who had never felt safe unless I was moving, moving, moving. When I was forced to be still, I was also forced to lay my resistance aside. I was forced to lay down the thing I'd defined myself by as a Black woman: my ability to be strong, to fight. And in my surrender, I was left with the quiet—and a quest.

Deep down, I knew my future work as a writer and educator would depend on my embracing this silence. Kevin Quashie wrote in *The Sover-*

eignty of Quiet, "The black artist . . . , if she or he is to produce meaningful work, has to construct a consciousness that exists beyond the expectation of resistance. . . . Quiet, instead, is a metaphor for the full range of one's inner life—one's desires, ambitions, hungers, vulnerabilities, fears. . . . Quiet is inevitable, essential. It is a simple, beautiful part of what it means to be alive."[1] To truly see my dreams come true, to have the vision of my life come to fruition, this was a truth I had to embrace. I needed to trust the silence to do its work.

God always had a plan for me. I just needed to be still long enough to hear it.

Then, of course, there was that nagging question asked of me by a very knowing therapist. "What does joy feel like in your body, Tracey?"

More silence.

I did not know the answer. I wasn't even sure I knew how to find it out. But the silence was compelling. It created a safe environment for me to unpack all my beliefs about myself, God, and people around me and to begin my own personal joy journey.

So, yes, reckoning with, accessing, and amplifying my joy began in the most unlikely of places: in the silence. I had to get still in ways I never had before so joy felt safe enough to make itself known. It had been crowded out for a long time. Other emotions and states of being had taken up significant space. Rage and grief and exhaustion were so big in my body, mind, and spirit that joy and love and peace could occupy only a tiny, minuscule corner of my heart. But the silence drew them out. As Renita Weems said in *Listening for God,* "I accepted the silence,"[2] and, in doing so, gave myself permission to hold all the joy I could stand.

That is what I hope the pages of this journal will offer you. A place for you to name and reclaim your joy. A canvas where you can paint the complexities of what it means to be a Black person in this world, with the understanding that we must always leave a little white space, a little margin for ourselves, especially when nothing but productivity and labor is deemed our lot. It's why I've chosen to include quotes from a variety of historical, sociological, and literary figures, some of whom may or may not be overtly Christian voices. I recognize that the truths found in all our lived experiences play an important part in how we understand, engage, and receive joy in our lives, no matter the faith tradition we claim. I pray that as you make your way through each entry, you give yourself room to move and play and restore what life has tried to steal from you. Even what you might have unknowingly given away.

That said, as a person of faith, I know and believe that above and beyond defining joy as a physiological response to pleasure, and *Black* joy as that same response housed within the specific historical and sociopolitical context that comes with being in *this* skin, ultimately joy is a person. Jesus embodies joy for us in the same way he embodies the more preached-about attributes of love and peace. And *that* joy has been a resurrecting power in my life. It is one I hope you see in your own.

As you journey through this devotional, you will notice there are more days spent exploring through guided prompts of what it means to know joy in our *bodies*. I've designed it that way. Our bodies are the starting points. When we can locate and recognize what joy feels like in our bodies—how much or how little space joy takes up and how our central nervous systems play huge roles in how we experience joy—only then can we move forward with creating more joy in our environments and relationships. In addition to those guided prompts, you will also find freewriting space in the Play by Play sections, where you can write down any feelings that come up for you each day and work out your joy plan in real time.

I invite you to approach this guided journal with intention, and as you take this journey with me for the next thirty days, I hope part of that intention will be to remember that joy is your birthright. We have an ancestral mandate not just to hold the pain and trauma of our experiences as Black people but also to hold the joy and love and peace that is ours too. In these pages, you are safe to explore joy and play and pleasure in a way that honors your lived experiences and expands them.

Welcome to your Black joy playbook! May your joy overflow in the most glorious ways.

—TMLG

JOY IN THE BODY

Day 1

REMEMBER THE OLD LANDMARKS

If you know whence you came, there is really no limit to where you can go.

—JAMES BALDWIN, *The Fire Next Time*

The roof was caved in on one side. With only two stone walls remaining to hold up what was left of the abandoned building, three entire floors were visible from the street. Church pews lay strewn about. Hymnal pages twirled loosely with every passing wind. An electrified metal fence ran along the perimeter of the property in order to keep both the curious and the criminal away.

It wasn't always this way. This used to be a place of worship. A sanctuary in more ways than one in this historic Black community. A place where women with graying hair and failing eyes still moved about the basement kitchen cooking macaroni and cheese, fried chicken, and pound cake to serve for the pastor's anniversary. Where deacons and ushers held vigil over congregants who stomped a hole in the floor with their shouting before being slain in the spirit. Where little girls in puffy tulle dresses and boys in tiny bow ties recited Easter poems with more confidence than correct pronunciation. Where choirs tore the roof off with their glorious praise. This church housed that unspeakable joy the hymn writer wrote about—the kind that not only glorified God but also bonded a community like nothing else could.

It had once stood strong.

Weathered, but strong.

All the while enduring the various environmental, political, and social seasons of the city—from wars and riots to migration and development. And now, many years after I first drove by that shell of a building, it is gone. Demolished and replaced by what some call progress. Nothing but a historical marker to note that it ever existed. Little evidence that joy—Black joy, in particular—ever lived there.

How many of us have places in our minds and hearts that stand as half-demolished monuments to our past? We hold memories of when we smiled and laughed freely and lived vibrantly, but now time has worn us down, obstacles have shown up, and we are finding it difficult to make our way back to who we once were. We want to know joy, but life keeps "life-ing," and we don't know how to make room for it.

I get it, friend. But here's where I want you to begin your work. Return to those glory days. Mine those memories. No matter what pain or hardship or destruction exists in your love or world, take yourself back to when you were a child and could access joy. Or maybe it was when you were a young twentysomething, ready to take the world by storm. Remember those giggles, those simple pleasures. As you do, allow your body to be immersed in those feelings. Pay attention to the tingles in your stomach and the warmth in your chest. Capture whatever it is your body is telling you about that joy. And once you've taken a snapshot of a joy long past, you can store it away and call it up when you need it.

CREATE YOUR OWN PLAYBOOK

Make a joy list. What were some of the fun things you did as a child—activities, toys, trips—that made you laugh or smile the most? Make a list of ten things, places, or events.

_____

_____

_____

_____

_____

_____

_____

_____

_____

_____

_____

_____

_____

_____

_____

_____

_____

_____

_____

_____

Reflect on *why* you think you enjoyed those activities.

_____

_____

_____

_____

_____

_____

_____

_____

When you call up the memories of these joyful moments (or if there is a recent moment of joy you can access), how does your body feel? Describe in detail here. (For example, *I get butterflies in my stomach when I'm experiencing joy. Not like anxiety, though. More like excitement. My chest feels warm. I feel light and tingly.*)

_____

_____

_____

_____

_____

_____

_____

*May I know that I can access
my feelings of joy anytime.*

Today I will choose joy by . . .

Turning on my favorite dance song (Beyoncé, Janet Jackson,
and Aretha Franklin offer great options for anthems!), setting the
timer on my phone for five minutes, and dancing my heart out.

Or . . .

(Fill in the one thing you'll choose to do today to experience joy.)

_____

_____

_____

_____

_____

_____

_____

_____

THE PLAY BY PLAY

Use this page to journal any additional thoughts or reflections that come to mind.

Day 2

EVEN IN THE SHADOWS, I SWING

Healing begins where the wound was made.
—ALICE WALKER,
The Way Forward Is with a Broken Heart

It was a hard day. One of the most challenging I'd had in weeks. Much of my work has to do with writing and speaking about the ways we Black folks have a right to our joy. We have a right to pleasure. But the truth is, there are many people who are resistant to this notion. Many who know that if more of us prioritize our joy, then some of the dehumanization we face will be ineffective.

Sadly, it's not just those outside the Black community who are resistant to our experience of joy. Sometimes it's us. Sometimes we mistakenly believe that if we make room for joy and pleasure, that somehow means we don't care enough about the hard things that are happening to us as a people. We think that giving ourselves permission to experience joy will somehow mean that the rage we feel at the injustices we face is unwarranted. Or that our sorrow and grief is somehow overstated.

But that's so far from the truth.

On this particular day, I'd worn myself out trying to say exactly that. I was feeling the weight of my work and was struggling to right-size myself in the middle of it all.

Whenever I get to the point of feeling down, I try to move. Movement is a powerful way to activate the parts of our bodies and brains that need to be soothed when we are frustrated, anxious, or sad.

Knowing this, I decided to take a walk around the neighborhood to clear my head and give my central nervous system a break. Walking is the one way I know to be present in the moment—one step at a time, one foot in front of the other—and force myself to breathe deeply so I can reset my mind and heart.

As I was leaving, my husband and daughter asked if they could join me on my walk, and of course I said yes. Because, in addition to movement, being in community with those we love is a good way to be present and work through any challenging emotions.

We threw on our sneakers and marched out of the house. After about a quarter mile, we came across our neighborhood playground and decided to stop instead of continuing around the mile-long circle that is our usual path. My daughter loves that place, mostly because it has a magnificent jungle gym, swings, slides, and a basketball court. Hubby and I agreed that it would be a good idea for her to get some playtime while we were out.

Well, I suppose it was not just for her. Apparently, Mama needed some playtime too.

I sat on the swings next to my daughter, who had already begun kicking and pulling her feet to make her swing go higher and higher.

I asked my husband to push me so I could match her height. As the swing began its climb, I immediately felt as if I wanted to cry. But these were clearly not tears of pain; they were tears of joy. I felt so light as I moved back and forth. It was as though a pressure valve had been released.

Eventually, our swings began to move in sync. The matched rhythm was absolutely thrilling for my daughter, who looked over at me and began rocking her Afro-puffed hair back and forth. Her giggles were contagious. I started laughing uncontrollably, the sound of my own cackles somehow pulling all that sorrow and rage out of my body.

And that was when it hit me! Swinging had opened the floodgates of my memories. I'd tapped into something—a kind of freedom, perhaps—I had been missing.

When I was maybe nine or ten, I loved to swing. As soon as I hit any playground, I'd make a beeline directly for the swings. And lo and behold, even at this big age, swinging had the same effect on me. I felt like I could touch the sky. Like I could fly. Like somehow through my own might, I could get closer to the face of God.

I quickly added "swinging on the playground" to my personal joy list.

Swinging makes me feel possible. Not just like *I have possibilities*, but that Tracey herself, with all her flaws and feels, is possible. My existence is affirmed in this simple act of play. I feel human. Real. But then maybe a little bit more than human. The act of swinging reminds me of what little Tracey once believed before her life taught her differently: that this journey through life isn't a fluke or a dream. That I can be brave and fearless, even when experiences say otherwise. The sound of the wind whooshing past my ears, the heaviness in my chest that weirdly also feels light, the spaciousness in my body as I pull myself higher—all these things remind me that in any given moment, I can choose freedom. The energy that surges in me when I'm on the swing is a powerful current that makes me feel like I can light up the world with one touch. With one word. And that's the point.

Maybe it's cliché to say that joy can set us free. But I promise you, friend, it really can. If you choose to "dance like no one's watching" in the middle of the day, it's inevitable that you will feel better. If you laugh with abandon at the characters on your favorite sitcom, there will be a release that happens. Our bodies are intelligently designed to process the joy they feel as good, and ultimately that leads to our mental, emotional, and spiritual wellness.

Sure, there's some science to this. Joy, at a very basic level, is a physiological response to pleasure. The euphoria felt can be attributed to the feel-good hormones dopamine and oxytocin that flood the body. But in light of the weight I felt in the moments leading up to sitting on that swing—the sorrow and rage that filled me as I read about another unarmed child being shot because he was Black, the unfiltered racism that showed up as I tried to do the work I feel led to do in a space that's too often resistant—I also realized that swinging was more than just a physical release for me. It was a vessel for joy to do its healing work.

CREATE YOUR OWN PLAYBOOK

Take a minute to reflect on how you might incorporate two items from yesterday's joy list into your current life. *(Did you list that you loved to sketch and design clothes when you were a teenager? Buy a sketchbook today or download a sketch app and reclaim that joy. Then write about how it feels to take that leap.)*

_____

_____

_____

_____

Let's take some of this inner-child work just a little bit further. In the space below, draw a picture of little you. No, I don't want to hear, "I can't draw!" None of that matters right now. Just give it a shot. Draw a picture of yourself. Have fun with it. Did you wear thick, chunky plaits like I did? Have a high-top fade? When you finish, I want you to look directly into the eyes of little you, drawn with your own hands, and speak today's meditation.

May I know that I am worthy of all the joy I can hold.

Today I will choose joy by . . .

Soothing my inner child. Maybe swinging at the park wasn't your thing.
Maybe you were a monkey-bars kid or loved to take on the biggest slides.
Why not stop at a playground and spend fifteen minutes playing?

Or . . .

(Fill in the one thing you'll choose to do today to experience joy.)

_____

_____

_____

_____

_____

_____

_____

_____

THE PLAY BY PLAY

Use this page to journal any additional thoughts or reflections that come to mind.

_____

_____

_____

_____

_____

_____

_____

_____

_____

_____

_____

_____

_____

_____

_____

_____

_____

THE ANIMATION OF OUR JOY

Hand Games (or When Black Girls Play)

**"Down, down, baby!
Down by the roller coaster."**

**"Miss Mary Mack, Mack, Mack,
all dressed in black, black, black!"**

One of the clear highlights of my childhood was when my parents said I was old enough to play with the big girls in our apartment complex. I was probably only seven and they were only twelve, but it felt as if a whole world opened up when I stepped into the courtyard and our portal of play. These Black girls and their ropes and chants and games were the embodiment of joy, filling my little heart to capacity.

In "The Magic of Black Girls' Play," writer Kyra Gaunt noted,

From backyards to schoolyards, their game-songs predate Emancipation. Their musical blackness has much to offer once we unpack the magic in the rhythms and rhymes that animate their torsos and release their tongues with laughter.

Games are [Black] girls' algorithms.[3]

In other words, even if no one else "out there" validated us, we mattered. With every hop, skip, jump, and sway, we mattered.

Day 3

YOUR BUS IS STILL COMING

We all have to stand on the earth itself and go with her at her pace.

—CHINUA ACHEBE, *No Longer at Ease*

I left my home as I always did that day, planning to catch a bus from Northeast Philadelphia to South Philadelphia, where I taught part-time at a nonprofit organization that served youth from marginalized communities. The bus usually stops a little after 11:15 A.M., and that day I was running a few minutes behind. I rushed out of my house, frantic, hoping I could still catch the bus.

I arrived at the stop and looked down the road, hoping it hadn't come already. After waiting about ten minutes, I realized that it must have and decided that instead of waiting forty-five minutes for the next bus, I'd walk to another stop and try to catch a different one. The walk between the two stops was about five minutes—ten since I was carrying a few bags that day.

Sounds pretty ordinary, right? Something thousands of people do every day.

Well, not quite. I'm always amazed at how God can turn the mundane into the extraordinary.

Here's the thing: As I was walking to the second stop, I found myself constantly looking back at the old stop. The one I'd just come from. The one where I'd clearly and definitely missed the bus. I suppose I was just double-checking. Making sure the bus that I already knew in my heart had passed wasn't going to magically come rolling down the street. I was so busy looking behind me that I ran smack into a tree branch. That's when I heard it: that small, still voice whispering its wisdom in my heart.

Stop looking back, Tracey. Focus on the bus you are trying to catch and not the one you've missed.

Whew! Isn't that it? How many times have we miscalculated the timing of something in our lives? It might not be a bus. Maybe it's a job opportunity or a relationship. For whatever reason, this thing didn't work for us and we are forced to move on to something that will. But instead of focusing solely on what it will take to get us to what God has coming for us, we keep looking back, doubting and questioning what's already been whispered as truth in our hearts.

We do this on our joy journeys too. We might have an idea of what brings us joy—which is fine as a starting point—but we soon realize that we are wrong. Yet instead of trying something new and stepping out of our comfort zones, we continue to attempt to force ourselves to get joy and happiness from that old thing.

Listen, friend, maybe your body doesn't like to party anymore! If that's true, stop going dancing every weekend. Believe what your body is telling you. Maybe it now loves yoga or nature walks. It's 100 percent okay to try something else. Your blessing is likely on the other side of that thing you're afraid to do.

Believe me when I say that constantly looking back at long-gone people, places, and things while trying to move forward in your life will slow your progress. If God had not brought to mind how my disbelief that the bus had already come was slowing down my current pace, it's entirely possible that I would have arrived at my new destination much later and even possibly experienced the consequence of missing *that* bus too.

In our pursuit of joy, there is also a need for balance. You don't want to keep looking back at what used to happen or who you used to be, but also don't rush as you move forward. Once I figured out that I needed to focus on getting to the other bus stop, I started walking really fast. I was almost jogging out of fear of missing that bus. I was rushing so much that I nearly tripped over my bags. When I finally arrived at the bus stop, I was sweating and out of breath, and my back was aching something terrible. Yes, I made it with plenty of time to spare, but guess what? The bus didn't move any faster. The driver didn't push down any harder on the gas pedal just because I'd decided to walk faster than necessary to get there. In fact, the bus arrived when it was scheduled to, but do you know who was looking a good and tired mess when it got there? Exactly.

There are two lessons here. First, stop looking backward at what you think you've missed. It's likely it was never meant for you in the first place. Second, just because you know your bus is coming down the road doesn't mean you need to rush unnecessarily to meet it. Keep walking in the Spirit. That's the pace God has designated for you. Be thankful for where you came from. Show gratitude for all the ways you survived the "missed buses" in your life. You are still here. Still walking this thing out. But don't rush it. Trust that you will reach your destination—wherever or whoever that might be—on time. That way, when your bus arrives, you are not stressed out because you tried to get there in your own strength. You can show up to that stop as the reflection of joy and peace you are meant to be. The things that God has placed in your heart as desires aren't going to move any faster just because you decide to rush it.

It may seem cliché, but it's true nonetheless: Be where you are. Don't hang back or move slower than you should in an attempt to capture what's long gone, but also don't rush ahead, trying to grab what isn't yours to have yet. Joy exists in your present. It is most accessible in your now. Too many times, we worry about what we didn't get to enjoy *back then*. Let's get this out of our systems. Let's find the joy we have access to *now*! Sure, we use the past to locate what joy feels like—an important exercise because our bodies are treasure troves of information. But our true reference point is the present day. What gives you joy today, my friend?

EXERCISE YOUR JOY

Take some time to map out how you are arriving at your present joys. In the spaces provided here and on the next page, mark the joys you have experienced in the past and the joys you have discovered along the way. Once you arrive at the point marked Present Joys, write a list of things that give you joy now. In the Play by Play section of this chapter, reflect on your journey so far. What have you learned about your joy journey? What do you hope to learn? What has changed for you?

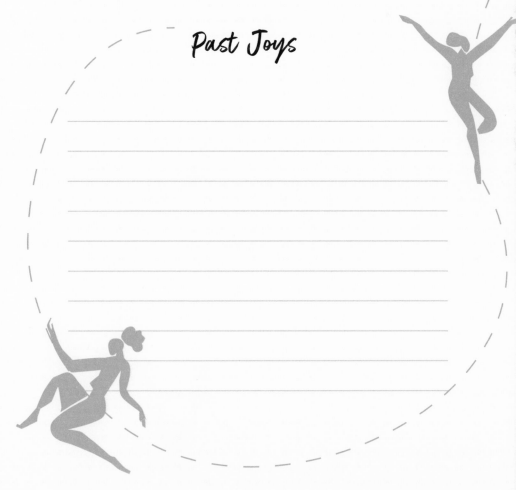

Past Joys

✕ Present Joys

_____

_____

_____

_____

_____

_____

_____

_____

_____

_____

_____

_____

_____

_____

_____

_____

May I remember I am exactly where I'm supposed to be.
I can pace myself and still reach my goals.

Today I will choose joy by . . .

Intentionally giving myself an extra hour to do a particular task.
I can start getting ready for bed an hour earlier, add an extra hour
to my dinner prep, or give myself more time on a project.

Or . . .

(Fill in the one thing you'll choose to do today to experience joy.)

_____

_____

_____

_____

_____

_____

_____

THE PLAY BY PLAY

Use this page to journal any additional thoughts or reflections that come to mind.

Day 4

THE FLIGHT OF
YOUR LIFE

*When I am constantly running there is no
time for being. When there is no time for
being there is no time for listening.*

—MADELEINE L'ENGLE, *Walking on Water*

If you travel often, you might have noticed that some flights are more active and entertaining or smooth and comforting than others. Whenever I get on a plane, I can often feel the energy of the people flying with me. Sometimes there's stress and anxiety in the atmosphere, particularly from those who have been dealing with delays or traveling with small children. An early-morning flight is often silent and peaceful, with many people sleeping or reading. Other times, like the day I flew to New Orleans with my girlfriends for the annual Essence Music Festival, there's joyful anticipation in the air. People on that plane—mostly Black women—were smiling and laughing and ready to have the time of their lives. (And we did!)

Isn't that just like life, though? Sometimes it's filled with laughter and joy, and other times the atmosphere can be so silent and still that we find ourselves wondering if everyone around us is asleep. In fact, a flight is actually a really good metaphor for how we can consider navigating this joy journey we're on.

Imagine your body, mind, and spirit as similar to an airplane. The first thing you should make absolutely sure of is who's flying the plane. If you are like me, as soon as you step onto the plane, you are assessing the captain. Listen, I need to make sure they look right! In the case of our lives, I think it's important to ask ourselves if God is truly the pilot.

I suppose you could fly yourself—there are many people who see themselves as the one in full control of their lives—but I prefer to be just a co-pilot. I'm on the flight deck, but I'm letting the One who is equipped with the proper knowledge, foresight, and vision run things. God knows our destination. The captain of a plane doesn't take passengers destined for Denver to Orlando. The only way we ultimately end up someplace we aren't meant to be is if we get on the wrong plane or if the wrong person is in the cockpit. God knows how high to take us and sees the turbulence ahead long before we ever do. And believe me, turbulence will come. All the more reason why I choose to surrender to God's control and navigation.

Bear with me as I extend this analogy a bit.

To me, the Holy Spirit acts as our flight attendant. The Spirit attends to our every need and provides comfort during our ride. But don't get it twisted! Like any good flight attendant, the Holy Spirit will also admonish us if we do something that is clearly against the guidelines of the captain (God) and the airlines (our own bodies). Additionally, this flight attendant of life will provide us with all the instructions we'll need to enjoy the flight. Yes, that might be the sacred texts of our faith, but it also might be observations we make of those who've taken this same flight before us. Our elders and ancestors are great resources. But how many of us even bother reading the instruction manual on a plane? I don't. Not always. Part of me figures that if something goes down, the flight attendant will tell me what to do. Another part of me thinks I don't need to keep reading it since I've heard it all before. In both cases, it's likely I will miss something that, if my life is ever at stake, is probably important to know.

The Holy Spirit, your flight attendant, is also the One who can speak to the Captain on your behalf. I imagine that pressing the little orange call button above our heads is much like prayer. We are alerting the flight attendant and the captain that we need something or that something doesn't feel right. We are seeking their guidance on what to do.

So, *what does this have to do with joy, Tracey?*

Glad you asked.

Just like a plane, your life can take you many places. On this particular journey, your destination is a fulfilling, all-encompassing, liberating joy. Yes, there are a million things you can do to get yourself there. But my life has taught me that allowing God to lead me on this journey is so much better than trying to figure it out on my own.

Do you know how many planes God has flown? Every single make and model since Creation. As a matter of fact, with God as our captain, we get the benefit of not just an experienced and certified crew but the creator and manufacturer of the plane itself. God knows the strengths and weaknesses of your particular model. God knows how much it can be pushed, when it needs more fuel, and when it needs to be grounded for maintenance. And because God undeniably wants to get us to our joy, there is no reason we can't trust that the Spirit will always be there, even in the midst of turbulence when clouds and storms shake and rock us.

Your journey to joy is no surprise to God. So sit back, relax, and enjoy the flight of your life.

EXERCISE YOUR JOY

Finish the following statements. Allow truth and curiosity to drive you.

I trust God to fly the plane of my life by

_____

_____

_____

_____

_____

_____

I trust the Holy Spirit to comfort me by

_____

_____

_____

_____

_____

_____

Spend some time in the Play by Play section reflecting on what you wrote above.

May I trust myself and the "crew" in charge
of getting me to my destination.

Today I will choose joy by . . .

Taking a walk when faced with something troubling. By removing myself from the situation, I can demonstrate that I'm trusting God to help me find answers so I can sit in peace with the uncertainty.

Or . . .

(Fill in the one thing you'll choose to do today to experience joy.)

_____

_____

_____

_____

_____

_____

_____

THE PLAY BY PLAY

Use this page to journal any additional thoughts or reflections that come to mind.

_____

_____

_____

_____

_____

_____

_____

_____

_____

_____

_____

_____

_____

_____

_____

_____

_____

THE ANIMATION OF OUR JOY

The Electric Slide

At nearly every Black family reunion I know of, there is one sound that is like a clarion call and unifies each person no matter where they came from: "It's electric!"

Marcia Griffiths's declaration in her 1983 remake of the Bunny Wailer hit "Electric Boogie" will always spark a mad rush to any open dance floor. And if not her Caribbean-inspired tune, then Cameo's 1986 smash "Candy" or Frankie Beverly's 1981 classic "Before I Let Go" will ensure it. While variations of the group dance known as the Electric Slide can be found in West and South African tribal dance, it's believed that the dance we all know now was originally choreographed by New York City dancer Ric Silver in 1976.[4] Those moves were later added to the choreography in Griffiths's song and ... well, here we are. The Electric Slide is an easy contender for the best dem-onstration of Black joy via movement, followed closely by any hip-hop dance born between 1980 and 1995.

Don't tell anyone Black you don't know how to do the Electric Slide or you'll be threatened with the revo-cation of the infamous Black card. And seriously, what would a Black joy playbook be without at least some guidance in that regard? So let me help you out a bit here so your Black card can remain safe in your wallet, purse, or pocket.

Remember, it's not necessarily as much about rhythm as it is about making sure you arrive at the end of each series of steps when everyone else around you does. Oh, and making sure you're facing the right direction. Turn the page for a cheat sheet that you can carry with you to the next wedding or family get-together. We're moving to the right first.

- **Take** four steps to the right. (Yes, there will be people around you who will double-time this. Ignore them . . . for now.)
- **Take** four steps to the left.
- **Take** four steps backward (with your body turned slightly to the right).
- **Stomp** forward once with your right foot.
- **Stomp** backward once with your right foot.
- **Kick**-step with your right foot and shuffle to the right. Then start again at the beginning (but now you are facing ninety degrees to the left from where you began).

Even if you don't get it, trust me, you'll still enjoy a few laughs while trying (as long as you keep your efforts in the back of the group and not in the way of Slide aficionados).

Black joy all around!

Day 5

ANSWER
THE DOOR

The truth is powerful and will prevail.
—SOJOURNER TRUTH

Truth is a funny thing. Most of us spend endless hours demanding it from everyone around us. "Tell me the truth. I can take it," we say to our friends. "Honesty is the best policy," we say to our children. We *say* these things because truthfulness and authenticity are the ideal. Yet when truth decides to knock on our front door, sometimes we are not inclined to invite it in. We don't say, "Hey, hard and uncomfortable truth. Come in and have a seat. You are welcome here." No, many times we slam the door in its face. We pretend we aren't home. Sometimes we even involve our children in the act. When they ask us about that thing knocking at our door, we tell them to ignore it. As a result, they grow up believing that if they ignore the truth, it will go away. The boldest among us just pack up and move. Running away seems so much easier than acknowledging our truth.

There was a time in my life when I was no different. I was a runner too. I loved the idea of joy. I could tell everyone around me about the benefits of it. Even when I couldn't articulate it all the way, deep down I understood that powerful healing was available to us through our immersion in joy. But somewhere along the line, a hard and ugly truth showed up: *Tracey, talking about joy is not the same as living a joy-FULL life.*

Whoa.

My inclination was to ignore this truth. Or run away from it. That was always my pattern anyway. I'd lived the life of a corporate salesperson when truth was calling me to write. I'd sold my happiness to the highest bidder with the largest cubicle. In other areas of my life, I'd built many a relationship on foundations of sand in order to maintain the facade of what I thought "having it together" looked like. And even throughout all this, truth was persistent. I had no reason to believe it wouldn't continue to be.

The thing about truth is, the longer you wait to face it, the uglier and bigger it gets. From past experiences, I know what that's like, so I decided not to wait around to see how much more that truth could press me. I heard it knocking, and I gathered up the courage to open the door. For me, that door was the need to shift from talking and researching and writing about joy to actually *living* what I was talking and researching and writing about.

I just peeked at the truth at first. Just to see. I noticed all the ways I was hiding and dimming my light because I didn't believe that the joy inside me was enough. I saw how I was comparing myself to other people and, as a result, allowing my joy to be stolen by the desire to have my joy look like theirs. Then I opened the door all the way. That's when I saw the chains. Because I wasn't allowing my joy full rein of my life, I wasn't as free as I claimed to be.

This truth was hard in my own home. See, I'd built my own world of comfort inside. Everything was beautiful. All the wrong existed outside my front door. But when I invited the truth into my home, reality struck with an incredible vengeance. Truth revealed the mess that existed right there on my couch when I removed the seat cushion. It exposed the trash that resided under my bed. It disclosed the furry green stuff growing on the walls inside my refrigerator.

The truth ripped off my mask and divulged my secrets.

But that was only the beginning. It was hard sitting in the discomfort of realizing that I'd not yet allowed myself to feel the fullness of joy. But once I got past that, I realized that truth is also a salve. A healing balm. It was showing me how different the life I was destined to live was from the life I'd been living. Truth found in my "house" things so old that I had forgotten about them. Like the reasons I resisted some forms of joy and the reasons that giving myself permission to have more joy felt unsafe. But once I saw things more clearly, I realized it was time to do the work.

Facing our truth helps us clean up the place. The spaces in our hearts and minds that are filled with all kinds of grief and pain sometimes need some decluttering so that we can make room for joy. Sometimes the reason we can't access joy is that we have too much stuff we're hiding from. Oh, but when truth knocks, go ahead and open the door, friend! It is a sacred healer. All that rage and sorrow will get rightsized and put in its proper place. Yes, the beginning of this process is challenging, but only because it's unfamiliar. But as soon as we invite the truth into our hearts once, it gets easier to keep doing it.

Give truth a key to your place. Watch how it gives you the strength to clean up the messes you've been ignoring or running away from. And then when everything is clear, watch how the thing you've been longing for—joy—has been there all along.

EXERCISE YOUR JOY

Write five absolute truths about your life right now. They can be positive or con-structive. By writing these statements, you are opening the door to truth in your life so that you can get about the business of growing the good and transforming the work in progress.

1. _____

_____

2. _____

_____

3. _____

_____

4. _____

_____

5. _____

_____

_____

*May I always welcome the healing
power of truth into my life.*

Today I will choose joy by . . .

Having a movie night. All this joy talk is a bit much.
Necessary, but a lot. I'm going to find a fun movie both
I and my friends love and enjoy a bit of fiction.

Or . . .

(Fill in the one thing you'll choose to do today to experience joy.)

_____

_____

_____

_____

_____

_____

_____

_____

THE PLAY BY PLAY

Use this page to journal any additional thoughts or reflections that come to mind.

BLACK JOY
MOMENTS IN HISTORY

I refuse to believe that some of my personal heroes lived without joy. In fact, I would argue that many of the historical figures we know and love (whom we rarely see smiling in photographs) definitely had joy moments. Things that made them laugh, dance, and sing but that also filled their hearts and spurred them on to do the work they did. It is Black joy that restored their faith in their callings, healed the places the world hurt, and gave them the resilience they needed to keep on keepin' on.

There is a wonderful black-and-white image of Dr. Martin Luther King, Jr., and actor/activist Harry Belafonte sharing what seems to be a boisterous, gut-busting laugh. While their conversation is likely lost in the ether of time, I often use what the preachers of my childhood used to call "the sanctified imagination" to ponder what might have caused them to laugh so deeply and with such joy.

"Oowee, the way I was sweating out there on the line? Whose idea was it to wear suits to the protest? I just knew I was gonna have to run by the cleaners and get a new shirt."

Okay, I'm sure those were *not* the words that sparked this exchange of joy and laughter between Dr. Martin Luther King, Jr., and Harry Belafonte. But no matter what inspired this interchange, it was clearly a moment of relief for two men who carried the weight of a people and a movement in their hearts.

If my joy doesn't look like that, I might not want it.

Day 6

EMBRACE THE PROCESS

When you recover or discover something that nourishes your soul and brings joy, care enough about yourself to make room for it in your life.
—JEAN SHINODA BOLEN

Many days I forget to choose joy. Because of this, I've come to recognize that it's easier to tell people they should write joy into every day than it is to encourage them to work through the challenges and resistance that will inevitably arise as they move through the process of reclaiming that joy. Two things can be true. First, I wholly believe that joy has the power to heal. I believe that when we're able to hold joy in tension with our other emotions, such as grief and rage, the lens through which we view our world and our lives becomes clearer. It's hard to see our way out of pain when joy is not part of the process.

That said, what's also true is that sometimes the unearthing of our joy is plain exhausting. This is especially real if you are coming from a place where you have rarely given yourself permission to experience joy or weren't taught how to be deliberate about having it in your life. Just like any healing process, you might find yourself saying, *Can I just be there already?* I get it. I really do.

This has everything to do with our perspective. If we believe that joy is a kind of healing but we regard healing as a finite destination, we will send ourselves into a state of fatigue. Healing is not a destination; it is a process. Every day is a new level to be explored.

I like to think of the joy journey as an adventure. It's where we learn more about what brings us joy and what doesn't, about how to be strategic in implementing our joy, and about all the various ways we can amplify other people's joy. It's not just a journey of a lifetime; it's a journey that will *last* a lifetime.

There's no pinnacle of joy expression to which we arrive. There just isn't. Joy isn't a place we get to. It's an existing part of us that we unearth. And just like with any healing journey, the days get easier the more we center joy in our lives. So much so that even when we have a bad day, our knowledge of joy—what it feels like, how it shows up for us—gives us the hope of knowing that the next day might be better.

It's too easy to get stuck, though. To decide on any random day that we will not choose joy because it feels like we aren't getting "there" fast enough. But again, that's the result of seeing this healing joy as a singular destination.

When we view our experience of joy as someplace "out there" we need to get to, we set ourselves up for disappointment. This is because when we find ourselves feeling as though enough time has gone by and that we should have arrived already but we haven't, we risk becoming devastated and giving up altogether. I am very intentional in calling this guided journal a playbook—not just because it's a way for you to document all the ways you can incorporate more play and joy into your life, but also so that in those moments when you're feeling exhausted or when the expression of joy doesn't yet feel instinctual for you, what you've written here can become a playbook much like the one a football coach might use. A coach uses the playbook as a place to house all the strategies the team will use to win—including the "plays" they will need to get out of a deficit. But that's where that analogy stops. It will be challenging to keep returning to this journal if you feel like your "plays" are there only for you to get to the championship, as opposed to a way to play the long game that is your life. Give yourself permission to see your joy journey as a lifelong healing process and then every step forward—and maybe even the ones backward—will be a win.

What if we believed that every single day was a new day to experience joy? And what if we focused just on the day we have in front of us—being present in our present—instead of on all the days to come? When it comes to our joy journeys, we don't have to project five years from now where we want to be. Capitalism and productivity mindsets tell us that we must have a five- or ten-year plan for everything. And sure, maybe we do if we want to buy a home or accomplish certain things in our career. But when it comes to our mental and spiritual well-being, that kind of thinking is deeply problematic. There is no five-year plan. It's about being present in the moment and allowing our bodies and minds and hearts to feel the healing power of joy. If we shift our thinking in this way, what will end up happening five years from now is we will look back over that time and see all these wonderful ways our life has been transformed by making joy the center from which we live.

Friend, let's embrace the process and begin to believe that healing is accessible right here and now. Even if it doesn't yet look like what we imagine or hope for.

EXERCISE YOUR JOY

There are two blank pie charts below. In the first one, indicate how much time you currently allot for joy and play. In the next pie chart, specify how much time you *desire* to devote to joy and play. In the Play by Play section, reflect on what you've uncovered here.

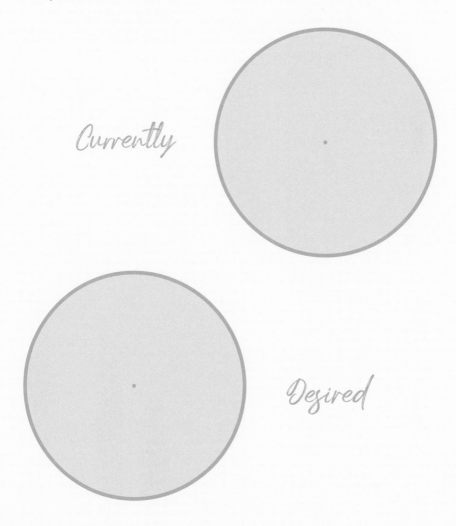

Currently

Desired

*May I accept my discoveries
of joy as a lifelong process.*

Today I will choose joy by . . .

Listening to a good podcast or reading a chapter from a book.
Sometimes I need to immerse myself in somebody
else's story to give my brain a break.

Or . . .

(Fill in the one thing you'll choose to do today to experience joy.)

_____

_____

_____

_____

_____

_____

_____

THE PLAY BY PLAY

Use this page to journal any additional thoughts or reflections that come to mind.

Day 7

LET IT GO

I listen for what's true. I release what isn't welcome.
—COLE ARTHUR RILEY, Facebook post,
#blackliturgies

I always make the vacation plans for our family. Generally, I'm the one who will do the research on hotel options and make the reservations for rental cars and plane tickets. So, you can imagine how I felt when I woke up the morning of my ninth wedding anniversary to my husband telling me that our original plans to take a quick weekend trip to Ocean City, Maryland, had changed.

Say what now?

I was surprised, yes.

Excited? For sure.

Anxious? Abso-freaking-lutely!

I mean, I'd done all the legwork! Lined up the hotel. Planned the spa services and made dinner reservations. My mom was coming up from Kentucky to Philadelphia to watch our daughter and we'd drive the two and a half hours to our getaway. You mean *all* of that had been changed?

Well, yes.

Little did I know that my husband had contacted my mother and orchestrated an entire coup, if you will. We were not going to Ocean

City. We were taking a much larger and more extravagant trip. And I would not be told where we were going until we arrived at the airport.

Airport?

As intriguing as this all was, I couldn't help but be in shock. My husband has never been the kind of person who plans vacations. *What if something goes wrong? Did he make reservations for everything we'll be doing? Did he use the right credit card? The one with the points?* My mind was moving at warp speed even as I was trying to zip my lips and roll with everything.

Then he handed me my ticket.

Miami?!

There were some bumps along the way. We ended up missing our flight, which I know frustrated him because we ended up getting to Miami later than he would have liked. Since it was a weekend trip, getting there even a few hours later interrupted his plans. But he recovered. And so did I. When we finally arrived, I learned that he'd rented a luxury car and that our accommodations were in a gorgeous hotel. Between massages and meals on our balcony, resting on the beach, and swimming in the clear waters, we had a glorious time.

Whenever I think about that trip, I'm reminded of the lessons it taught, the primary one being, *You can let go, Tracey. You don't have to be in control all the time.* For me, always being in control is a way to be safe. It is essentially a trauma response. If I'm doing it, then I know it's getting done to the standard that I like and I don't have to worry about something going wrong. And in the unlikely case that something does go wrong, I can implement the five thousand contingencies I have in place. As bananas as that sounds, the truth is that too many of us are living just like this.

Hypervigilance and extreme control are joy stealers. Yes, for all the obvious reasons, but mostly because in being overly controlling or anticipatory, we forget that we are worthy of care and ease. We are worthy of someone else handling the business. We are worthy of rest. Of not always having to be "on." Of not always managing, producing, and administrating. There is joy in being cared for and allowing someone to take the reins and let us chill.

For some of us, the blocks we have in experiencing joy are rooted in one truth: We don't know what it feels like to be cared for. Because of this, joy (and the liberating feeling of it) comes across as unsafe. We are badly triggered by a person's care for us because it is unfamiliar and therefore uncomfortable.

I often talk about my challenges with relaxation. Whenever I begin to relax, when I choose joy and settle into it, my body tends to react negatively. In addition to feeling anxiety, I experience chronic pain or some other physical sensation that tells me there are parts of me that are deeply uncomfortable with my ease. It's like they are saying, *Wait one second now, Ms. Thing. Remember the last time you relaxed like this? X, Y, and Z happened. This feels the same as that time when you let your guard down. You are not in control right now, which means you are leaving yourself open to bad things happening.*

Sound familiar?

Black people are especially prone to hypervigilance, and rightfully so. We have enough on the record to fuel our belief that if we don't pay attention, if we relax too much, if we make the mistake of resting or embracing ease, then we will inevitably succumb to the racist systems that are already designed to not support us. So, despite the fact that we desperately need more joy, peace, and ease, we resist them because our collective muscle memory says they're not safe.

My body operates in the same way. Even since beginning my healing journey and gathering a boatload of tools to help me navigate my past trauma, I still experience my body's resistance. Those parts of me continue talking: *No ma'am. We are going to stop all these relaxation shenanigans. Let's make these muscles tense up. How about a headache or toothache?*

So, what exactly do we do about it?

First, we continue to use our tools. Feeling anxious? Ground yourself with deep breathing and movement. Prayer and meditation have been amazing in helping me settle into the acceptance and trust I know I need for any given situation. Body hurting? Consider holistic pain management like acupuncture and a massage. And beyond the physical manifestations of your hypervigilance, work toward releasing your need for absolute control.

Too many times, the things we're attempting to control are things we actually can't. It might be hard to hear, but there's no amount of control we can wield that will stop a bad thing from happening. And exerting that extreme control can prevent us from experiencing joy. Let's work on surrendering our hypervigilance and embracing care and ease, even if it's just in bite-size doses, and watch how that makes room for more joy in our lives.

EXERCISE YOUR JOY

I don't know about you, but one of the times I feel the freest is when I'm listening to music. I once had a friend call me the "human jukebox" because I tend to know all the lyrics to most songs that play on the radio, regardless of genre. I also love to make up songs. My daughter rolls her eyes daily as I sing, "Let's get up and do your chores. Sister, go and do your chores. If you want to go outsiiiiiiiiide."

Yes, it's that serious.

So, let's have a little fun. Today you are going to write your own joy song. This will be the song you sing when you need a little boost to your day. If you are musically inclined, feel free to create your own melody. Or you can choose an existing melody to set your song to. I've helped by providing the first or last words for the verse and some guidance in the chorus.

Title of Song: _____

Verse One:

_____ joy

_____ time

Give _____

My _____

Chorus:

_____

_____

(repeat first line)

_____

_____

May I release some control and let go of
what is keeping me from my joy.

Today I will choose joy by . . .

Sharing my joy song with at least one other person.
You never know! I might just start a band/group.

Or . . .

(Fill in the one thing you'll choose to do today to experience joy.)

_____

_____

_____

_____

_____

_____

_____

THE PLAY BY PLAY

Use this page to journal any additional thoughts or reflections that come to mind.

Day 8

TO BE LOVED

*Love takes off masks that we fear we cannot live
without and know we cannot live within.*

—JAMES BALDWIN, *The Fire Next Time*

I heard God say, "I love you," today.

And while I knew this is not new information,
   I did hear it differently than I ever had before.

This time it was personal.
This time it was intimate.

Almost like it was our special secret.
   A special secret for a special girl,
   A secret that made my day-to-day fire walking
      much more tolerable,
   And possibly, definitely worth it.

It was like God knew me—really knew me.
Knew me enough to know that I needed to hear that.
Knew me enough to know that my ability to have joy
      depended on hearing that.

In fact, I think I might have prayed that very thing.
"Show me you love me."
"If joy is a person, make it plain."

And my prayers were answered this time.

This time.

God answered in that voice.
A voice separate from my own but still the same.
    In the still of an early morn,
    When all was quiet on my block,
    When humankind had failed at showing me what
        I was so desperately looking for—

Agape.
    Pure and unadulterated pleasure
    And maybe, most of all, peace.
    The voice of the Spirit responding to what felt
        broken inside,
    What I'd been unable to fix.

Oh, the joy of those words!
The joy of being loved by One who *knows* you
        knows you.
And to respond.

With every bit of sincerity in me,
    Hanging on the edge of my slumber
    As the dawn of a new day sought my undivided
        attention,

I said, "I love you too."

And for the first time in my life, my heart sang
        and swelled because
I believed.

EXERCISE YOUR JOY

In the space provided below, draw a picture of your favorite toy as a child. What memories of love does the toy spark? Spend some time in the Play by Play section of this chapter to explore how thinking about that toy makes you feel.

May I always know and feel I'm loved.

Today I will choose joy by . . .

Calling someone I haven't spoken to in a while
and telling them I love them.

Or . . .

(Fill in the one thing you'll choose to do today to experience joy.)

_____

_____

_____

_____

_____

_____

_____

_____

_____

_____

THE PLAY BY PLAY

Use this page to journal any additional thoughts or reflections that come to mind.

Day 9

SURRENDER TO THE MOMENT

You have turned my mourning into joyful dancing.
You have taken away my clothes of mourning
and clothed me with joy.

—PSALM 30:11, NLT

Just like her mother, my daughter is 100 percent a beach baby. As soon as she got over her natural awe of the ocean and figured out it wasn't necessarily going to swallow her whole (a real question she had), she was all in. At four years old, she sat at the edge of the shore and played in the sand. Now twelve, she's all about her boogie board. There have been more times than I can count when I've had to literally drag her out of the water or force her to eat some food because she'd stay in all day if I let her. She loves it that much.

I get it, though. I, too, am drawn to the water. Simply looking at a body of water calms me in a way that I'm sure some scientist or doctor can explain better than I can. That's why it does my heart good to see how much my daughter enjoys the beach. Since my family recently moved to the shore with the specific purpose of being closer to the water, it's been a blessing to be able to pop over to the beach and enjoy some sunshine whenever we want.

One summer day, in a moment of both gratitude and desperation—yes, it was *that* kind of day—my husband, daughter, and I made our way over to our local beach to relax and bring down our stress levels. As soon as we hit the sand, my baby girl threw off her cover-up and ran straight into the water. The look on her face as she ran through the waves was everything! Her smile and laughter are always beyond infectious, but this day she had that twinkle in her eye that novel writers often use to describe a character's joy. But this was no cliché. This was real! And I was seeing it firsthand. She giggled as she continued to dive in and out of the water, and I had this sensation that felt like nothing else was going on in the world except what was happening in that moment with her.

This is the kind of freedom I envy. This idea that you can be so present in your life that what has happened in the past and what might happen in the future are only distant memories or vague contemplation. This way of being so . . . here. So part of the now that you allow yourself the liberating experience of being completely overtaken by joy.

I remember filming her and (because she's a total ham) expecting her to do what she usually does, which is stop and pose. But not this time. There was no posing. Just this pure connection with nature. I went back to my chair next to her dad and watched as she flipped and cartwheeled along the edge of the shore. That's when the tears came. I cried because I longed for that kind of freedom.

Even as I write this, I find myself longing to be in a mental and emotional space where, for a consistent period (forever?), the stuff of my past isn't intruding upon my thoughts. As someone who lives with post-traumatic stress disorder, I often feel as though I will never get to the point where I'm not constantly aware of how my body is responding. Not to what's actually happening in the moment—oh no. What it *thinks* is happening from years prior.

So, to see anyone, including my child, enjoy that kind of freedom of movement and thought really is a point of reflection for me.

I'm so happy for her. And because I'm on my own joy journey, I took advantage of what she was teaching me. In a less organic but still very fruitful way, I put my phone down, tore off my cover-up, and ran into the water with her. I played and splashed and let the water push me over. Yes, I am a Black woman, and yes, I got my hair soaking wet. I was willing to do anything for joy.

I have hope that there will be a day when joy does not come in fits and spurts or as a result of observation but will pour out of me in waves. I know I'm close. And maybe you are too. Together, we can work on surrendering. Because that's what this really is, right? What I observed in my daughter that day was her surrender to the moment.

I encourage all of us to find ways we can completely surrender to the experience of joy. All we have is the moment we're in, so let's allow ourselves the space to breathe deep and be overtaken by the joy that wants so much to show us how worthy we are of it.

Part of the work of joy, the essence of play, is to learn how to surrender to the moment. To be present. As with most things, if something is unfamiliar to you, it will take intentionality and planning to catch your rhythm. To let your body know that this thing, this feeling, is okay and safe. That's why I say to write joy into your day. To schedule that ten-minute dance break or go jump on the swings at the park. You can choose not to allow the chaos of the world to encroach on the moments you set aside. And eventually what was once planned and intentional becomes normalized in your body, mind, and spirit and you find yourself surrendering to joy whenever and however it shows up.

Create a sacred boundary around your joy moments. Whether it's something spontaneous and organic that just happens or something you've crafted and planned, be present and aware enough to observe that your joy moments must be protected at all costs. That is how we can give ourselves permission and room to surrender to the joy.

EXERCISE YOUR JOY

What does surrender look like for you? What makes you feel the most free?

_____

_____

_____

_____

_____

_____

List three areas of your life—places, people, or situations—that you would like to protect because they are sacred spaces of joy and peace for you. Be very specific. In the Play by Play section, reflect on how you might create a boundary around those three areas.

_____

_____

_____

_____

_____

_____

_____

May I choose freedom as I'm present in my joy.

Today I will choose joy by ...

Connecting with water in some way. If you live near an ocean, lake, river, stream, creek, or pool, go and sit by it for at least fifteen minutes. If you don't, take a bath or hot shower and be intentional about paying attention to how you feel as the water rushes over you.

Or ...

(Fill in the one thing you'll choose to do today to experience joy.)

_____

_____

_____

_____

_____

_____

_____

THE PLAY BY PLAY

Use this page to journal any additional thoughts or reflections that come to mind.

_____

_____

_____

_____

_____

_____

_____

_____

_____

_____

_____

_____

_____

_____

_____

_____

_____

_____

Day 10

ENSURE YOUR HARVEST

Our bodies are our gardens, to . . . which our wills are gardeners.

—**WILLIAM SHAKESPEARE**, *Othello*

I first became interested in gardening about fifteen years ago. My husband and I were renting what Philadelphians call a row house, which is simply a kind of townhome that's connected to other townhomes. We had a very small patio and a patch of grass—and that was it! But because we were newly married, I wanted to do something that made our house feel more like a home.

So I decided to get some seeds and grow a couple of tomato plants. The first harvest was small, but I wasn't deterred. Every year, I'd try to grow something in that space, and every year, we got more and more tomatoes. I didn't know much about gardening at that time, but I still felt compelled and fascinated by the reality of growing my own food and by all the lessons that gardening could teach me. I loved the idea that when it came to gardening, I could succeed or fail epically and everything would be okay. Much of my life at that time felt pressurized. There was an expectation to do well, whether that expectation came from myself or from the people around me.

I was caught up in this season of hyperproductivity—busy, busy, busy—that, in the end, kept me exhausted and unwell. I felt an overwhelming amount of pressure to meet some arbitrary standard set by society and myself. But with this new hobby, this new joy of mine, I could make mistakes and it was still okay.

After a few years, we moved on to buy our first home together. It was what Philadelphians call a "twin," which is another type of town house that is connected to just one other town house. We ended up living there for ten years. Because we had a little bit more space, I expanded my gardening repertoire to include potatoes, cucumbers, and squash. I built three raised beds and had numerous containers filled with veggies.

One year I decided to grow several squash plants. I was so excited as I watched the huge vines grow and the yellow fruit begin to flower. About halfway through the summer, I started noticing these little black dots on the backs of the large leaves. I didn't think too much of it at first, and I didn't do anything about it. I figured, *Oh, that must just be part of the leaf.* Over time, though, I started to see more black dots, but again, I didn't address it. I don't think I even researched what the dots could be.

A few weeks later, I went out to water the plants and found bugs everywhere. It was like they had shown up overnight. That's when I tried to spray them with a variety of organic pest-control products. Nevertheless, my glorious squash plants—with their huge, green, furry leaves—completely wilted and were eventually devoured by the bugs within a span of a couple of weeks. I was devastated. We ultimately had to pull them out of the ground and get rid of them all.

As crushing as this experience felt, I must admit it was also a wonderful lesson that I suppose only my gardening could have taught me in that season of my life. The primary message was this: Address your problems head-on. Sometimes what we allow to steal our joy the most are things we have ignored for way too long. Situations and circumstances and emotions we've pushed down deep and decided not to deal with. Instead of confronting our problems or choosing to deal with the stuff interfering in our lives, we decide we can't handle it. We put it aside, not realizing that the longer we wait, the bigger our challenges can get. To the point where, when we do decide to deal with things, we have to yank everything up by the root because the damage is too far gone.

This is especially true when it comes to our inner lives, spiritually and emotionally. When we choose to ignore the emotions that show up in our bodies—the anger, the frustration, the grief—those things become rooted. They can, if we aren't careful, devour us. We can easily become people who lose their great outlook or kind spirit and instead become defeated. All because we didn't address the source of our pain. Moreover, the fruit of the Spirit—joy—gets lost in the process. Like my squash, what once was glorious and filled with potential becomes unusable and completely ruined.

Had I just read a little bit about the types of things that show up on squash leaves or even reached out to other gardeners for guidance, I would have quickly learned that those black dots were the eggs of squash borers. At the bare minimum, I could have cut the infected leaves or knocked the eggs off or sprayed the plant with neem oil to prevent the eggs from hatching. But because I didn't do any of that, I lost the whole harvest.

Friend, I don't want you to lose the magnificent harvest of joy that awaits you. Address the inevitable conflicts, challenges, and troubling emotions that come up. Deal with them now so you don't have to deal with them later.

EXERCISE YOUR JOY

Name them: What are three primary conflicts you're currently facing in your life?

1. _____

2. _____

3. _____

Feel them: What emotions come up when you think about these conflicts?

1. _____

2. _____

3. _____

Address them: Write at least one way you can deal with/resolve/manage each conflict.

1. _____

2. _____

3. _____

May I take the needed actions to protect my joy.

Today I will choose joy by . . .

Buying a small indoor plant to tend. I will call her Joy, and I will tend
to her in all the ways I tend to myself on this joy journey.

Or . . .

(Fill in the one thing you'll choose to do today to experience joy.)

_____

_____

_____

_____

_____

_____

_____

_____

_____

_____

THE PLAY BY PLAY

Use this page to journal any additional thoughts or reflections that come to mind.

Day 11
THE ULTIMATE MOTIVATION

Somebody once said we never know what is enough until we know what's more than enough.

—BILLIE HOLIDAY, *Lady Sings the Blues*

"I just want this to be done already!" I said as I stared at my therapist through my computer screen. My frustration was not a reflection of the work she'd been doing with me. I'd been in therapy regularly for the past seven years, with the last four being with this particular practitioner. She was and is amazing.

I think I was just tired. Exhausted and exasperated with the process of healing. I was drained from feeling as though I'd make a little progress, only to see myself facing the same challenges. Like the elders in the Black Baptist church of my childhood used to say, I'd be "walking the straight and narrow path" and then something would trigger me and I'd "backslide" into old patterns.

Being in therapy and doing the hard work of digging up my traumatic experiences—examining where joy was seemingly missing, discovering where I lacked peace and why, and implementing tools to manage my life—was difficult. It was often too hard to see my growth.

Thankfully, my therapist is unmovable whenever I have these wild and indignant proclamations. She calmly received my words and then redirected me to the truth.

I am not who I used to be.

I am not who I desire to be.

I am becoming.

"The fact that you are even aware of and can locate the gaps in your healing is progress, Tracey."

She was right. There was a time when I didn't know what I didn't know. I didn't know there was a lack of joy in my life. Or, rather, I didn't know I had permission to have joy; I thought I had to work for it. I couldn't even locate joy in my body, much less create a plan for it in my life.

Now it's different. I not only know what joy feels like, but I know how to reach for it when I'm overcome with other big feelings. But the one thing I learned that day as I grumbled at my therapist was that healing is not a destination. There is no "there" for me to get to. There is no time in the future when I will be able to throw my tools out the window. As I grow, I certainly may not need them as much. But living life on life's terms—choosing to accept the ups and downs, ins and outs of how life unfolds—means realizing that triggers will inevitably come and that it's imperative to think of tools (breathing, grounding, prayer, meditation, soul care) as modalities that are part of a lifelong practice. Healing is, by far, a process.

Which makes sense, right? If it took me more than forty years of operating the way I previously did, with no tools, to even get to a place where I could see that I had an issue, why in the world would I think that I could "fix" all that in six months or even six years? Why am I trying to fix it at all? That's just not how any of this works. Getting to healing, getting to your joy, takes time.

We can slow down, friend. Move with ease through this journey. Pace ourselves. We don't have to rush. We don't have to put any undue pressure on ourselves to be at a certain place in our lives that we haven't reached yet.

I remember when I first began writing about Black joy. Some people struggled with my approach. The expectation was that I would focus on all the animations of our joy as Black people across the Diaspora. They wanted me to center my work on the music and art and culture. The ways in which we show up in a place. The special-ness of us. And listen, I'm here for all that! I write about all that. But what I found was that I didn't really *need* to highlight those outward demonstrations of joy. Yes, they are important parts of the resistance, a way to humanize us within systems intent on our dehumanization. But what I found even more powerful were the ways we used joy for our own healing. I became curious about how we, individually and collectively, have been able to hold and amplify joy amid great pain. How we have been able to use joyful moments and actions as memory markers in order to heal and restore ourselves. I want to know what lay underneath our elders and great-grandmothers' cries of, "This joy I have—the world didn't give it and the world can't take it away." Because underneath any demonstration or animation of our culture is the deep, sustaining undercurrent of joy that helps us keep going when we just "want this to be done already."

That's not to say we don't hit a wall sometimes. That's real. You might have read all the books, listened to all the gurus, been in therapy for X number of years. You might be working hard to acknowledge patterns and implement tools that will hopefully create new neural pathways and facilitate change. But then you just stop. Because it's hard sometimes. And tiresome. And the world out there can be as uncooperative as it can get with the process of your joy journey. Just remember that part of accessing joy is realizing that even when you're at your most exhausted, when you're at your most exasperated with the process of healing, there is something that can keep you going. Joy is truly the best motivator. When you can be intentional about experiencing joy, then it will motivate you to keep going when you get to that wall. The joy will remind you of why you're doing the work in the first place.

EXERCISE YOUR JOY

As you might be able to tell, I believe in the connection between our bodies and our minds. Both science and my own lived experiences support this. Sometimes our bodies will reveal to us where the gaps are on our joy journeys.

Below are three simple acts of joy. Under each one, write how the act might motivate you to keep going.

Taking a thirty-minute nap

_____

_____

_____

_____

Walking through grass barefoot

_____

_____

_____

_____

Stretching for five minutes in the morning and evening

_____

_____

_____

_____

Today's Meditation

May I embrace how far I've come.

Today I will choose joy by . . .

Downloading a language app and beginning the journey toward speaking a new language, with five minutes of practice each day.

Or . . .

(Fill in the one thing you'll choose to do today to experience joy.)

_____

_____

_____

_____

_____

_____

_____

_____

THE PLAY BY PLAY

Use this page to journal any additional thoughts or reflections that come to mind.

THE ANIMATION OF OUR JOY

Spades

I lifted my body slightly out of my chair while simultaneously holding the card high. I imagined myself akin to Michael Jordan as he floated through the air and dunked the ball. Only it wasn't a ball I held. Dare I say it was something greater? Something known to send a room full of people in all shades of brown into the emotional stratosphere.

High above the square black table with its folding legs and four lightweight chairs, high above both the head of my teammate and the stunned and salty visages of my competitors, I held . . . the BIG JOKER.

I flicked that bad boy down onto the table with such finesse that even the memory vibrates with my sauciness.

Quieting my shenanigans a beat, I actually whispered my next words. Because, of course, I ain't showing off or nothing.

"Y'all set."

If there was ever a flagship game of Black American culture—a crown jewel of home entertainment, if you will—it would be the card game Spades. No, we are not monolithic as a people, so there are—gasp!—Black people in this country who do not know how to play. But there are enough participants on record to say that from college dorm rooms to Saturday-night house parties, Spades is a game revered by many in Black American culture.

Day 12

BEAUTY AS A PORTAL TO JOY

Beauty is not in the face;
Beauty is a light in the heart.

—KHALIL GIBRAN,
"The Sayings of the Brook"

I've always been drawn to beauty. When I was younger and my parents, little brother, and I lived in an apartment (they had not yet bought their first home), we used to drive through the wealthier neighborhoods in our town. These suburban mini mansions were usually part of an annual Homearama event that showcased high-end landscaping and furnishing. My parents would drive through the neighborhoods and point out various things they liked and disliked about the homes. My dad might comment on the practicality of the two-car garage or muse on what the mortgages might cost. My mom might remark on the design of the front door or how great it was that the backyard was fenced in.

Looking back, I know this was a way for my parents to cast a vision for themselves. A way to dream about the kind of home they wanted for our family. But I just remember riding in the back seat, ponytail or plaits swinging, and being captivated by the lawns of these homes. The flowers and gardens were spectacular, and every space looked so beautiful. And peaceful. Deep down, I aspired to one day have a space that was exactly that: both beautiful and peaceful.

As a teenager, my attraction to beauty took a different shape. I always wanted to be friends with the pretty people. I wanted to be around people, places, and things that were aesthetically beautiful to me. I was the one who went on field trips to museums and stood in front of art pieces for the longest time trying to "figure them out."

By that time, I was also heavily influenced by society's beauty standards. I looked to the wrong people for explanations of what made something worthy of being called beautiful. I focused on the surface-level, tangible things. Hip-hop told me what made a woman beautiful. The way someone's hair lay. The size of their nose and lips. The media—television and film in particular—taught me what it meant to have a beautiful life.

Unfortunately, for a young Black girl growing up in the South, those standards rarely ever aligned with what I saw in the mirror. Yes, I had a myriad of beautiful Black women around who countered what I saw and offered balance to my burgeoning perspective, but they seemed to be struggling as well. I'd long detached from the feelings of peace that beauty formerly inspired in me. It would take many years and lots of counseling to unravel what I'd spiritually ingested and return to wanting a beauty wrapped in tranquility.

Thankfully, I have now recovered much of my childhood appreciation for beauty. In fact, as I write this, I am sitting at a lake near my house. The light waves in the water are moving in concert with one another. A current is moving west on the lake, and every tiny wave is in beautiful alignment with the one next to it. And then the trees:

I'm convinced there are at least a million shades of green present in my line of sight. It excites me, this revelation.

Joy percolates just under my skin as I watch the symphony of nature. And then I get it. The beauty I'm experiencing in this moment isn't necessarily about what I'm seeing. It's not about the waves or the color of the trees. It's about this feeling I get while seeing it all. It's about being open to the sensations that spark the realization that *this is beautiful.* That's when beauty truly makes its presence known. It's why someone can sit at this very lake, watch this very water, see these very trees, and feel absolutely nothing. Because they haven't opened their minds and hearts to the possibility of beauty—or they don't know how to.

That's the cheat code. So much of what we call beautiful is simply what's aesthetically pleasing, or "easy on the eye," as my elders used to say. But true beauty is a portal to joy. It's connected to the way a person, place, or thing makes you feel.

Part of the work for all of us is recognizing that if we take a moment to sit with what's truly beautiful, we will open the door to joy. Joy is, at its core and as I mentioned earlier, a physiological response to pleasure. When we admire something we believe to be beautiful, it's often aesthetically pleasing first. So it's a good idea to take a beat and meditate on the emotions that come up for us in that experience. How does that person, place, or circumstance make us feel? Do we feel pleasure in its/their presence?

If you are struggling to access joy in your life, maybe start by embracing beauty. Pay attention to it when it's nearby. Be still long enough to feel what it does in your body. If you can find your beautiful, then you can access your joy.

EXERCISE YOUR JOY

Take some time to look at yourself in the mirror. Really search your face and body. Don't turn away. Ignore those voices of critique. Just look at yourself. Now smile with your whole face. Not a grin or smirk. Show all those teeth. I promise, no one is looking.

Seriously, go do it right now.

You're back? Great.

Now write five things you find beautiful about what you saw in the mirror.

1. _____

2. _____

3. _____

4. _____

5. _____

In the Play by Play section of the chapter, reflect on the observations you wrote here and consider how seeing your own beauty might open you up to more joy.

May I look for the beauty that exists all around me.

Today I will choose joy by . . .

Wearing something I absolutely love but haven't worn in a long time.
I will dig into my jewelry box for those earrings I got for Christmas or
pull those shoes out of my closet that I haven't worn in forever.

Or . . .

(Fill in the one thing you'll choose to do today to experience joy.)

_____

_____

_____

_____

_____

_____

_____

_____

THE PLAY BY PLAY

Use this page to journal any additional thoughts or reflections that come to mind.

BLACK JOY
MOMENTS IN HISTORY

Writer and activist Audre Lorde once wrote, "The sharing of joy, whether physical, emotional, psychic, or intellectual, forms a bridge between the sharers which can be the basis for understanding much of what is not shared between them, and lessens the threat of their difference."[5] I think she understood this more than most. There's another fantastic image, emerging from the annals of history, that shows Lorde in a canoe or kayak, holding the oars, her face tilted toward the sun, and her mouth wide in unapologetic Black joy. Every time I see it, I say, "Look at that smile!" Lorde got it! She understood that if we want to embrace our own powerful, restorative, resilient joy, there is so much we just might have to let go of. Joy is our pathway to liberation. Freedom loading . . .

JOY IN THE BREATH

Day 13

BREATHING THROUGH THE RESISTANCE

*We need joy as we need air. We need love
as we need water. We need each other
as we need the earth we share.*

—MAYA ANGELOU, Facebook post

For as long as I can remember, I've resisted being in my body. Allowing myself to feel, to be present in my body, has always been a challenge. And when I say "being in my body," I'm really talking about being present. I'm intoxicated by the life of the mind. Being in my head. There I can make up stories about what is or isn't happening. I can be in the past or the future and not have to deal with what I'm feeling in the moment.

I know that some of this has to do with the personal trauma I carry. It can be challenging for those of us with hard pasts, especially from our childhood, to be in our bodies, because we are scared of what that is like. We feel as though we are out of control. Being present to the emotions and feelings that come up in us as a result of our reality exposes us. More than anything, we fear the vulnerability required to stay in our bodies. To stay present.

Because I'm someone who has used control to remain safe, choosing to return to my body and allowing myself to truly feel what I feel has been critical on this healing journey. It's way too easy to push away rage or downplay my sorrow. But when I do this, I actually allow those emotions time and space to become bigger and more ingrained. I think I am exercising my control, when in reality I am creating fertile ground for the hardest of these very natural emotions to take root. Yet when I can sit with those emotions without judgment, feel them in their entirety, I actually am allowing those feelings to pass through me instead of getting stuck. Yes, it is the hardest healing work of my life, but I must do it.

Why, Tracey?

Well, joy exists in the present. If I want joy, I have to be present to experience it.

But the resistance is real. I want to acknowledge that. You may have even found yourself battling the resistance as you move through this journal. The parts of you saying, *You are wasting your time, Joy is subjective,* and *You don't deserve joy after the life you've had*—yeah, that's the resistance.

But don't ignore it. Listen to it. I know that sounds counter-intuitive, but hear me out: Those resistant parts of you have formed as a result of your actual life experiences. In their own way, those voices think they are keeping you safe. Vulnerability is a risk they are not willing for you to take. Choosing joy is a risk they don't want you to take. Acknowledge that. Tell the parts of you that are scared of choosing joy that you hear them and understand where that fear comes from. Do this in the same way you'd acknowledge the fear of a child who is scared to ride an escalator. The same way you'd hold their hand and help them through it. You have the ability to tell those resistant voices inside, who are most likely the younger parts of you, that you understand that choosing joy is unfamiliar and scary but that you will walk them—yourself—through it.

Then . . . choose joy anyway.

It's really a choice. Yes, fear seems like an immovable weight, but really it's just a combination of all the ways your body and mind have tried to protect you as you've lived life. Had a good experience? Your body says, "More of that, please!" Had a painful experience? Your body says, "No, thank you!" But you ultimately get to decide when to hit the override button. Because as important as your body and mind are, your spirit matters also.

So, when I feel the resistance rising up in me, I choose to navigate through it. I remember joy is on the other side of my being present.

Returning to my body looks like returning to my breath. I spent many, many years (nearly forty) shallow breathing. Yes, like literally not taking any deep breaths on a regular basis. It's actually more common than you might think. Take a minute right now and breathe.

In through the nose for *one* . . .

Two . . .
Three . . .
Four . . .

Now exhale through the mouth for *one* . . .

Two . . .
Three . . .
Four . . .

Let's do it again:

Inhale JOY, two, three, four . . .
Exhale pain, two, three, four . . .
Selah.

When was the last time you actually did that—took a deep breath?

For so many of us, it's been a while. Grind culture and society's constant demand for productivity has led to our not even noticing how little we are breathing. When I realized this about myself, I was more than dismayed. By cutting off my air supply, I was making my body work harder for oxygen that should have just been readily available to me by deep breathing. In turn, my shallow breathing was having all kinds of effects on the way my muscles and organs were operating.

So, when the resistance comes, I have conversations with the parts of me that are unhappy with this new journey I'm on, and then I breathe. Accessing joy (and, ultimately, healing) begins when I allow myself to take the breaths I need. I breathe . . . and then realize that I'm not going to fall off the face of the earth because I missed one workout. I take another breath . . . and then realize that I have the power to not allow someone else the room and space to hurt me. And when the deep breathing causes an emotional reaction in me—because breath work can "bring up some stuff"—I reach out to those who can support me and talk through my feelings.

That's important too. Because whatever you put in place as a response to the resistance that might show up when you decide to choose joy, having people you trust and with whom you can talk through things is always a good idea.

Deep breathing also allows my body and muscles to relax. Recently, I've been working on my relationship with my belly. For the longest time, I'd been socialized to believe that holding my stomach in all day and night was just what women with thicker bodies had to do. Well, deep breathing doesn't allow for that. I've had to wrestle with the parts of me that believe that by letting my stomach fill with air, I'm somehow leaving myself open for harm. So I breathe again . . . and then realize that, in this particular moment, no one is coming for me. No one can hurt me. I can be safe and relax.

Here's the caveat to that. Because I'm someone who has lived through personal experience with racial gun violence as well as observed it happening all around me like the rest of the world, there is absolute logic to my body's hypervigilance. My body regularly says, "You can't let your muscles relax and release too much, because we are in an environment where something could harm you. You could go to the grocery store and not make it home. You could be standing in your yard and be killed for simply being."

That's so real.

Yet I choose to breathe deeply anyway because of this one hard, hard truth I've embraced: Whether relaxed or not, I have no way to stop anyone who is intent on harming me.

Whew! Painful, right? Yes. But the reality that many Black, Brown, and Indigenous people live in is that if someone's going to attempt to hurt or harm or even kill us, our not relaxing, our tightening of our muscles, and our operating from a place of fear is not a shield. It's not going to stop that bad thing from happening. So we might as well choose joy. We might as well choose relaxation. We might as well breathe.

There is conflict in me, even as I write this. Because I know that feeling safe really is the genesis of truly experiencing joy. If we're always hypervigilant and we rarely feel safe, it's going to require extra work for us to allow our bodies to experience the kind of joy that's connected to freedom and liberation. But that's our work. That's why we are working through this Black joy playbook together. Choosing joy means daily giving ourselves a taste or glimpse of what it means to be free. Maybe it starts with our breath. Or releasing the tension in our muscles. Or poking our bellies out. Or talking ourselves into doing something new and unfamiliar but good for us—salsa dancing, anyone? Maybe this is how liberation comes.

EXERCISE YOUR JOY

Our breath is affirmation. Our breath is grace. Every breath for a Black person is a dynamic testimony in a world hell-bent on stealing our lives whether through actual execution or the slow burn of dehumanization. Breathing deeply is a demonstration of our defiance. There is nothing that defies white supremacist power structures more than the deep, cleansing, affirming breath of joy from the people they marginalize.

Just for today, set five alarms on your phone, computer, or alarm clock. We will call these your breath breaks. When the alarm sounds, I want you to take ten deep breaths in the manner I've presented earlier in this chapter. At the end of the day, take time in the Play by Play section to reflect on how you felt. Did breathing deeply and with intention help you? What emotions, if any, arose when you took your breath breaks?

May I always remember that I have my breath.

Today I will choose joy by . . .

Putting together a meal-prep plan. Preparing meals ahead
of time is a great way for me to get ahead of any exhaustion
that might show up in my week.

Or . . .

(Fill in the one thing you'll choose to do today to experience joy.)

_____

_____

_____

_____

_____

_____

_____

_____

_____

THE PLAY BY PLAY

Use this page to journal any additional thoughts or reflections that come to mind.

Day 14

GOD IS PLEASED WITH YOU

You make known to me the path of life;
in your presence there is fullness of joy;
at your right hand are pleasures forevermore.

—PSALM 16:11

Most mornings, I sit in my garden, my office, or even just a chair in my bedroom and pray and meditate, usually adding some journaling to the mix. I often begin my journal entries the same way many of us do: I pour out my thoughts in a stream-of-consciousness fashion. I write about my desires and longings. I write about specific events in my life and how they are affecting me. Inevitably, though, about halfway through my journaling session, I experience a shift. A change in a point of view. At that stage, my writing is less about me sharing my heart in my journal and more about the Spirit speaking back to me.

One day, I was sitting on my patio, pen and journal in hand. Most of what I was writing that day was about wanting to do and be better. I felt like I wasn't "getting life right." I kept messing up.

Kept doing what I knew didn't work. I wanted to correct some things in my life and didn't know how to do so consistently. At one point as I was writing, I felt this overwhelming frustration. But it wasn't *my* frustration exactly. It was like I was sensing someone else's frustration with me. Of course, I assumed that this was my feeling just how much God was upset with me. I started to cry. The tears fell hard and fast. Then I picked up the pen and wrote these exact words:

Why is it so hard for you to believe that I'm pleased with you, Tracey?

Wait, what? The frustration I was feeling wasn't an indication that God was ashamed of me; it was a kind of exasperation of the Spirit because I wasn't seeing just how much God loved me. How pleased with me he was. And that's when the feeling in my body changed. It was like every limb became warm, and light filled my chest. Joy was there.

Believing that God was actually pleased with me, that the Spirit was walking with me and transforming me daily, and that I didn't have to worry about every rule I'd break along the way because my heart was always turned toward God was an utterly strange concept. The traditional and ultimately bad theology of my childhood had taught me something else. My own poor and twisted understanding of who God is and how he functions in my life was also a huge contributor. I'd found myself striving to please a God who could never be satisfied. I thought I needed to be perfect to be blessed.

Life confirmed this for me too. Easily into my early forties, I didn't believe I was enough. This perception of being perpetually unworthy caused me to constantly perform for the love and acceptance of people, even to my own detriment. I beat myself up about the smallest of mistakes. I gave zero room for my humanity and lived at the extremes. I was either supermom or a horrible parent. The best writer in the universe or someone who should throw her laptop out the window.

And, of course, I transposed how I dealt with people onto God. Surely, he would require even more from me than them, wouldn't he?

My grace is sufficient for you.

Ah, grace. What a concept.

I'm reminded of a conversation I had with my daughter once. She asked, "Mommy, do you love me?"

"Of course I do," I said.

"No matter what?"

"Yep, no matter what."

She thought a bit, then asked, "Even if I do something terrible?"

"Even then."

Next it was my turn to think. I said, "There is nothing you can do that will make me not love you. Even as you experience the consequences of your actions, I will still love you. Because I'm your mom."

Why wouldn't that apply to you, too, Tracey?

It finally clicked. Part of my joy journey was truly accepting God's love. Truly believing I'm worthy of it. Because how can any of us truly embrace the fullness of joy if we don't allow ourselves to receive love from our creator and then from those who have been called to love us? Yes, life will hold me accountable for my shortcomings and mistakes, but even then, nothing can separate me from the love of God (see Romans 8:38–39). That truth has been life-changing.

I now imagine God as a proud, loving parent. As a God who, like me with my tween daughter, gets frustrated with my shenanigans but never stops loving me. A God who sees me trying and is pleased to call me his daughter.

Look at you, out here living and whatnot!

As my elders used to say, God is "pleased as a peacock" with me and this life I'm making. Not because I am perfect or have been the most obedient. There is no amount of piety that earns more of God's love. And I'm so flawed in many ways. Human. But still, I am and you are the imago Dei—made in the image of God. And there's joy in this realization. Because everyone has access to God's pleasure.

I know that church folks love to throw around this notion of being "favored by God." Sadly, I think many confuse the favor of God with being his favorite. That's not a thing. As children of God, we all have access to his favor. When we do justice, love mercy, and walk humbly (see Micah 6:8), we especially feel the light and warmth of God's pleasure. And *that* is available to everyone.

EXERCISE YOUR JOY

In the boxes below, create your own three-panel comic strip. The theme will be "Conversations with God." Draw and tell a story that captures your view of what your talks with God look like.

Conversations with God

May I know and feel God's pleasure.

Today I will choose joy by . . .

Resting. If possible, by sleeping in or otherwise, I'm going to give myself an extra five, fifteen, thirty, or sixty minutes of rest.

Or . . .

(Fill in the one thing you'll choose to do today to experience joy.)

THE PLAY BY PLAY

Use this page to journal any additional thoughts or reflections that come to mind.

THE ANIMATION OF OUR JOY

Graduation Day

"That's my baby!"
"That's what I'm talking about, Son!"

It doesn't matter if Little Man is graduating from pre-K or if Baby Girl is finishing her doctorate, Black folks are going to celebrate, and celebrate loudly, during a graduation ceremony.

There are rules, I guess. I imagine that most administrators find themselves a little perturbed as they stand on the platform and say, "Please hold your applause until the end of the presentation," knowing full well that no one is paying attention. And if the student population is significantly Black, yeah, Grandmama and Uncle Joe don't even hear them.

I love that we believe in celebrating our wins big and loudly. Mostly because I know that the joy that's demonstrated at these events runs deeper than the stereotype of Black folks just loving to be loud. It's a carryover from a time not long ago when our wins were hard-won. When even the idea of graduating from high school or college made the "cap-and-gown day," as one family member of mine called it, feel as though a huge mountain had been scaled.

When we think about the way our educational and economic systems can often prevent Black people from attaining those goals—maybe because of poverty or because a student is first-generation and doesn't have any real academic support or models—it makes sense that graduations are where we're able to let loose and release our joy at what a family member or friend has accomplished. Their joy is ours. Their win is ours.

Day 15

CHECK YOUR ENVIRONMENT

In every crisis there is a message.
—SUSAN L. TAYLOR

Some of the biggest impediments to experiencing and accessing joy are things we don't think too much about. Maybe we're doing all the right things. We've identified what joy feels like in our bodies. We've made our joy lists. We've been intentional about creating moments of joy consistently. But maybe we are still struggling because we haven't paid much attention to who or what is in our space. Environment matters, and sometimes the blockages we feel when trying to live more joyful lives come from surrounding ourselves with people and places that drain us.

Have you ever gone into a room or met with a person and then, though you might have had a perfectly fine conversation or experience, walked away with something feeling off? Me too. And what I've come to learn is that nine times out of ten, the sirens blaring in my mind and gut are simply the Spirit making me aware of something. It rarely ends well when I don't attend to what my discernment reveals.

The energy (or "vibe," as Gen Zers call it) a person brings to a space can shift and change the atmosphere. It can bring you down to the point where even if you're doing something you truly enjoy, you might have a hard time tapping into the deeper joy available to you in the moment because you feel a weight you can't quite place.

So, how can you become more aware of your environment?

The first step is to evaluate how you feel when certain people are in the room. Does that friend have a spirit of encouragement, or do you always feel like a loser when they are around? Is that family member the type of person who makes a room brighter and lighter when they enter it, or does it feel dark and heavy while they are there? Some people leave a place better than they found it. Others use words and ways of being that are always negative and critical. When it comes to the latter, it's a good idea to think about whether those people are worth having around you, especially if your intention is to live a more joyful life.

The challenge with this is that sometimes those who are weighing us down are loved ones. What do we do when the ones we believe are preventing us from really experiencing joy the way we want are family members, a spouse, or that bestie we've had forever? It isn't easy to remove ourselves from those relationships, and, to be honest, we may not want to entirely.

I get that. And this is where I think we must consider what emotional distance looks like in those situations. We can have people in our lives who are physically present but with whom we've created boundaries that prevent them from emotionally affecting us. Yes, Mom can come and see her grandbabies. No, Mom cannot comment on the choices you make in running your household. Yes, your girlfriend is welcome on the girls' trip. No, she doesn't get to gossip to you about your other friends while there.

Inevitably, we will experience pushback when we set these boundaries. Doing so may or may not require or lead to a conversation with the person. I believe in the redemptive power of relationships and know that it's entirely possible that "guarding your heart" (see Proverbs 4:23) could lead to another person's transformation as you become a mirror to them. But I also have heard so many stories about the opposite happening. So you must be clear from the beginning about your expectations. Check your environment and set boundaries for your own well-being. Be ready for whatever the outcome may be. Do not emotionally distance yourself from a loved one as a way to manipulate them into changing. It rarely works, anyway. There's a singular goal when checking your environment: to preserve and keep your joy safe.

EXERCISE YOUR JOY

Make a list of five individuals or places that have challenged you over the past decade. I encourage you to just sit with those names for a bit. Offer up a prayer for each person or place and have a candid conversation with God and yourself about the steps you should take. Do you release them from your life totally, do you have a conversation about the boundary you're setting, or do you simply begin to distance yourself emotionally? Reflect on this in the Play by Play section of the chapter.

1. _____

2. _____

3. _____

4. _____

5. _____

May I be willing to investigate my environment.

Today I will choose joy by . . .

Spending time with two or three people I've identified as kind
and supportive individuals in my life. Maybe it's lunch with a group
of friends who make me laugh. Maybe it's a work session with
others in my field who support my dreams.

Or . . .

(Fill in the one thing you'll choose to do today to experience joy.)

_____

_____

_____

_____

_____

_____

_____

THE PLAY BY PLAY

Use this page to journal any additional thoughts or reflections that come to mind.

Day 16

IN MEMORY
OF . . .

*Love is not at the mercy of time and it
does not recognize death.*

—JAMES BALDWIN, *Just Above My Head*

My grandmother Viola Brown was complicated. And beautiful. And fabulous. And saucy. And tall. With gorgeous black hair and beautiful chestnut skin. Granny was fly and fierce-tongued. She knew pain but also joy. She knew heartache but also love. She had her demons but knew God. She lived in North Carolina and Virginia. And Kentucky. And New York. And Italy. Her laugh sounded like a waterfall, if waterfalls were made of gold. She loved plants and coffee and beer and Star Trek and handsome men. She loved the color red and silver jewelry. Oh, and me. She loved me. I was her joy, and she was mine.

Wait . . . and cobbler too! She loved peach cobbler. She made it the old-fashioned way and the quick and dirty way. I'll share the latter with you because . . . well, the former? We could never. Turn the page to make the cobbler for yourself.

Viola Brown's Peach Cobbler "in a Pinch"

2 small cans or one large can peach chunks (if 4 cups of fresh are not available)

1 2-pack pie crusts (uncooked)

1 cup sugar

½ cup flour

1 tsp cinnamon

1 tsp vanilla extract

3 tsp melted butter

Grease a casserole dish with 1 tsp of butter.

Take one of the two thawed pie crusts and put it inside the casserole dish, fitting the dough along the sides.

Mix peaches, sugar, flour, cinnamon, vanilla, and melted butter in bowl.

Pour mixture in casserole dish and place the second pie crust on top.

Pierce the top with a fork multiple times.

Place small pats of butter on top.

Bake at 350°F for 45 minutes or until golden brown.

"But you've gotta keep checking it."

—MY MAMA
(VIOLA'S DAUGHTER)

EXERCISE YOUR JOY

In the space below, write a letter to a family member who has passed away. Share your heart with them. Tell them all about this joy journey you're on.

Dear _____,

_____

_____

_____

_____

_____

_____

_____

_____

_____

_____

_____

_____

_____

_____

_____

_____

_____

_____

May I always honor those ancestors who made a way out of no way for me.

Today I will choose joy by . . .

Pulling out old pictures of me with loved ones who have passed away.
Allowing myself the freedom to feel all my feelings.

Or . . .

(Fill in the one thing you'll choose to do today to experience joy.)

_____

_____

_____

_____

_____

_____

_____

_____

THE PLAY BY PLAY

Use this page to journal any additional thoughts or reflections that come to mind.

JOY IN THE TEARS

Day 17

GRIEF IS NOT THE WHOLE STORY

Even the darkness is not dark to you.
—PSALM 139:12

It was Good Friday, the holiday that many Christians celebrate right before Easter (or what some believers refer to as Resurrection Sunday). Good Friday is the religious event that commemorates the moment when Jesus was crucified, which ultimately sets the stage for his resurrection on Easter morning.

On this Good Friday, I was sitting in my garden, praying. It had been a heavy week, and I just needed to be still. Inevitably, I started thinking about what Good Friday meant for me and allowing myself to sit with the weight of the implications. I kept coming back to this notion of the day being "good." How could this awful, terrible thing that happened to such a proponent of love and grace and redemption be a good thing? Sure, I knew what *good* meant theologically from the standpoint of my faith tradition. We have the privilege of a post-resurrection vantage point. But I also understood how diminishing it feels, how painful it is, for someone to dare call my grief *good*.

I am acutely aware that when I talk about joy, Black joy in particular, and explain the idea that we can and do hold both pleasure and pain, joy and trauma, simultaneously, some people might interpret that as my diminishing the latter in favor of amplifying the former. In essence, it might sound like I'm attempting to make grief or injustice "good." So I had to sit with that for a little while. I needed to work it out in my mind.

Here is where I landed:

What transforms pain into power, what made the sacrifice of my Messiah a gateway to goodness, was the understanding—dare I say, the *knowledge*—of first-century and present-day believers that grief was and is never the whole story. We (especially oppressed people) unquestioningly have the capacity to hold in tension both the grief and the good in our lives. Yet, clearly, embracing the overlap in the present moment is challenging, healing work. We struggle with identifying and naming the good amid the grief, and yes, even in identifying and naming the grief amid the good. Remember how tough it's been to claim joy when it seems like you are experiencing nothing but chaos? Exactly.

Thankfully, the grace revealed in this joy journey is that we, over time, learn to be in our pain and still sense that resurrection is coming. In simpler terms, keeping joy in the mix helps us maintain hope. For my Black ancestors, hope was a critical piece of their resilience strategy. They—and I, if I open my heart to it—were able to hold the pain and violent lived experiences of racism and white supremacy in the same space with their joy. As a result, joy became a conduit for their hope, which kept them alive when everything around them wanted to kill their bodies and spirits. As poet and novelist Paul Laurence Dunbar once said, "Hope is tenacious. It goes on living and working when science has dealt it what should be its death blow."[6]

When we choose joy, we have hope this "trouble won't last always," as my elders used to say. We have hope that the pain and grief of our stories are not the only chapters in this thing called life. We know that the particulars of our present pain might not be able to be changed, but we believe a new experience is possible. It's why we continue to march and protest. It's why we continue to fight for what's right. Because we still believe change is possible.

My prayer is that you, too, will do what my ancestors did: Keep your eye on the resurrection that's coming. I know the job situation looks dead. I know the relationship looks lifeless. I know that your mental health looks hopeless. But choosing joy, every day, in any way you can, is a kind of defiance that makes room for hope to spring eternal. Transformation and transition and reclamation and liberation are possible. No, choosing joy doesn't make grief feel good. But it does remind you that you are still here and, therefore, you can keep going.

EXERCISE YOUR JOY

This is your hope tree. In the middle of grief, keeping hope on the horizon is always a good idea. Especially since we know that the more joy we give ourselves permission to feel amid our sorrow, the more our hopes come alive. Write the hopes you have on the fruit of this tree and then reflect on them in the Play by Play section at the end of the chapter.

May I know and feel that grief is not the whole story.

Today I will choose joy by . . .

Buying or picking myself some flowers. I will bring them
home and put them in water. I will then take a minute
each day to observe and smell them.

Or . . .

(Fill in the one thing you'll choose to do today to experience joy.)

_____

_____

_____

_____

_____

_____

_____

THE PLAY BY PLAY

Use this page to journal any additional thoughts or reflections that come to mind.

Day 18

BUT YOU STILL GET TO GRIEVE (WITH A PURPOSE)

I may not be there yet, but I am closer than I was yesterday.

—MISTY COPELAND

We can hold both grief and joy in our bodies, but another side exists to that idea. For some of us, we use joy as a way to not grieve at all. We're *always* acknowledging the joy and never the pain.

I'll never forget a review I received about my book *Black Joy: Stories of Resistance, Resilience, and Restoration*. The complaint boiled down to the fact that the reader did not want to wade into pain and trauma to hold the joy. They didn't want to read about that at all. They wanted the funny parts. The cultural signifiers. The laughter. They didn't want to think about the trauma in which all those wonderful animations of our joy live.

I get it.

It's the same argument people make about watching "slave" or "hood" movies. They say they don't want to watch another film about the enslavement or poverty of our people, because they feel like, for too long, that's all that existed.

I get that too.

But I'm not sure we get to Black joy by cutting ourselves completely off from the experiences that make our joy Black. We must be willing to grieve even as we laugh. It is possible to achieve a harmony that doesn't require erasure.

For example, I've recently had to grieve the fact that the version of myself that existed ten years ago is not coming back. I will never be that Tracey again. Still, throughout my personal healing process, there have been times when I wish I could go back and retrieve pieces of myself. Times when healing felt like a weight and a responsibility. It's like I hear the late, great Maya Angelou saying, "When you know better, you do better," and part of me wants to go back to the time when I didn't know better. So I wouldn't have to do better. So I don't have to be compassionate to that person. So I don't have to pull out my tools when panic and anxiety set in. I can just wield my anger destructively like I used to. I can just sink into the darkness like I used to.

But, clearly, that version of myself from ten or twenty or thirty years ago is never coming back, because I do know better. And even as I choose joy every day, I get to grieve that. I get to say that there's a part of me that became familiar with my pain and figured out how to navigate the world with my trauma intact. I get to recognize that though I am healing, though I'm embracing my joy, I'm also struggling a little bit because this new thing is unfamiliar; this experience of joy feels different. I get to have my own Good Friday, if you will, for the versions of myself that I know have to die in order for me to resurrect and become who I need to become.

I like the word *transition* that's generally used in Indigenous cultures when someone passes away. I like it because it implies a change of form but not essence. My loved one isn't gone forever; they've just taken a different form. It's a change of the vessel but not the spirit. Their essence, the thing that allows me to hold my memories of them, remains.

So, whether it's Jesus on the cross, as discussed in the previous chapter, or a version of myself that has to die in order for me to live in my purpose, there is some usefulness to be found in our pain. Not that the pain is good—it isn't. But God is the ultimate alchemist, transforming our pain into power, working it out for our good. It doesn't mean that the old version of myself doesn't have value; it means that I've just taken a different form. The Tracey who went through that bad thing, the thing I could have surely done without if it were up to me, still informs who I am becoming. Death, physical or otherwise, is not an ending but a beginning. By virtue of what resurrection does for us—remember, it gives us hope—well, that's the ultimate power of joy.

EXERCISE YOUR JOY

Write an obituary for a previous version of yourself that has "transitioned," or passed away. If you want to take this exercise a bit further, invite close, trustworthy friends and family to a ritual or ceremony where you finally lay that former part of yourself to rest.

May I give myself permission to grieve
even when joy is present.

Today I will choose joy by . . .

Giving an elder a call. Maybe one of my parents.
Or grandparents. Or a member of my fraternity or church.
Sometimes speaking with someone who's lived a bit can offer
me wisdom and perspective on this journey.

Or . . .

(Fill in the one thing you'll choose to do today to experience joy.)

_____

_____

_____

_____

_____

_____

_____

THE PLAY BY PLAY

Use this page to journal any additional thoughts or reflections that come to mind.

BLACK JOY
MOMENTS IN HISTORY

Toni Morrison dancing in a lounge in early 1980s New York City. James Baldwin "cutting a rug" with CORE worker Doris Jean Castle in 1963. Maya Angelou regally two-stepping with Amiri Baraka in 1991. Every one of these moments of joy is documented in photographs widely shared on the internet. Every one of them gives us insight into the full lives of my literary ancestors. These were all legends who lived and loved, and lived some more.

Black history is not comprised solely of stories about trauma and tragedy. It isn't just about what happened to us and what we've been through; it's also about the story of joy. Even the most renowned voices in our history and culture laughed, danced, smiled, and got their joy on. Let them be a reminder that no matter the struggles or successes, you can make room for joy in your life. No need to measure your joy against these images. Comparison is truly the thief of joy. Just figure out what your joy looks like and do it with as much vigor as possible. In the words of Beyoncé, "You are the bar."

Day 19

JOY IS
UP THE WAY

Joy is not made to be a crumb.

—MARY OLIVER, *Devotions*

I didn't think too much about the trees when we decided to move to the woods. I was excited about moving out of the city, closer to the ocean, and I knew I wanted a couple of acres of land. I desired enough space where I could feel expansive, as expansive as the land itself. I also wanted a place where my daughter could feel free to run around. Where she'd have the space to play and really tap into the joy I know nature can deliver. But I didn't think about the trees specifically. And, trust me, there are a lot of them.

We have a sunroom where I often sit and just stare out at the trees, which are impossible to miss. They are everywhere. Some are relatively small, ten or fifteen feet at best. The majority are huge, easily a hundred feet tall or more. And they surround our property.

One winter day as I was sitting on the porch, drinking hot tea, I found myself trying to do what I've been telling everybody else to do: access a little joy since things were feeling tough. A familiar depressive episode had come upon me, and I was pulling out all my tools. I'd already been praying, deep breathing, doing yoga, writing in my journal, getting massages, and swinging on the tire swing my husband had hung from one of the largest trees, but frankly, nothing was working. The darkness still hovered. Apparently, I just needed to be still.

Sometimes the singular thing joy requires of us is to sit with the feelings we have and allow them to be. Yes, it's good to call up joy when we can, but there are inescapably going to be moments when we are unable to even do that, because of how deeply embedded the emotions of grief or anger might be.

I was having one of those days. I just couldn't tap in. Sitting there, wrapped in a weighted blanket, tea cooling very quickly, I looked out into the woods behind the house. Everything was so barren. The trees had no leaves, and the weeds and vines looked brittle and lifeless.

And that's when it came to me.

If I didn't know any better, I could sit in that chair and assume it was impossible for those branches to ever see any green. That those vines would never swell and grow. Based on the evidence in front of me, I might have thought that everything in those woods was dead forever. But I did know better. I knew spring was only a few short months away. I knew that even as I was looking out at such stark barrenness, such desolate, dry, and seemingly dead places, there would also come a time when the entire wood would be rich with green leaves and plants. The trees and bushes would bud and then flower. Life would return.

Why would my life—or *our* lives, for that matter—be any different?

Yes, I was struggling with accessing joy in that moment. But that didn't mean it wasn't "up the way," as my Kentucky elders might say. Life was requiring me to sit still for a moment. But my sitting wasn't without hope; the darkness hovers, *and* I can sit with the anticipation of joy.

Even when the tears won't stop and the way is unclear, allow yourself the gift of hope, my friend. Holding on to hope might not be easy, but doing so prevents you from sitting too long in the hard place. Hope ensures that you will see joy when it arrives and be able to run out to meet it. Hope is that proverbial light at the end of the tunnel, the glint of possibility in your peripheral vision. It's the knowledge that you've been here before and that no matter what this moment looks like, joy can come in the morning. Even if it's not tomorrow morning, it's coming.

As you're navigating this playbook and putting together your plays, account for the days where nothing will work. Then trust that your spring is coming. There will be greener, brighter days ahead. Life awaits.

EXERCISE YOUR JOY

Set your alarm for fifteen minutes. Go someplace quiet where you won't be interrupted at all, and just sit still. Don't worry about all the thoughts in your brain. Just let them come and go. The goal is just . . . stillness. That's the exercise.

Today's Meditation

May I trust that joy is near even when I can't see it.

Today I will choose joy by . . .

Finding five to ten minutes of quiet each morning this week.
Maybe that will mean waking up a little bit earlier or taking a
breather in the car before heading into the office. Regardless,
I will find a way to begin my day without all the noise.

Or . . .

(Fill in the one thing you'll choose to do today to experience joy.)

_____

_____

_____

_____

_____

_____

_____

THE PLAY BY PLAY

Use this page to journal any additional thoughts or reflections that come to mind.

_____

_____

_____

_____

_____

_____

_____

_____

_____

_____

_____

_____

_____

_____

_____

_____

_____

Day 20

THE WEIGHT OF JOY

We are the [people] of the dance whose feet only gain power when they beat the hard soil.
—LÉOPOLD SÉDAR SENGHOR, "Prayer to Masks"

Growing up in a Black church in the South, I became fluent in the language of church. There is a clear cultural lexicon that's part of my experience and one I'll never forget, no matter where my faith journey takes me. It includes call-and-response, which is when an audience affirms a preacher by talking back to him aloud. There's the "Amen!" and "Hallelujah!" But there's also the "You better preach!" or "Bring it home, Pastor!" It's a beautiful rhythmic dialogue partially born from West African drumming traditions.

You might know other recognizable phrases, even if you didn't grow up in the church. Mostly because it's the same language that shows up in most Black settings. Whether at a juke joint, a concert, or the church house, if someone is singing their tail off, it's likely the audience will respond in kind.

"You better sing!" is a phrase often followed by a wave of the hand and facial expressions of disgust—though not to be viewed as a bad thing. More like an acknowledgment of how utterly moving the singer's voice is. (See *ugly cry*.) Again, this dialogue between speaker/performer and audience is equal parts confirmation, communication, and connection.

One of my favorite "calls" in the church is when someone says to a preacher, "Walk heavy, Pastor!" or "You're talking heavy now." It makes me imagine the prophets of the faith from way back and their actual, physical posture. I've always presumed there was a weightiness to the way they moved. What I love about this imagery, what that heaviness implies to me, is that these people were grounded. Yes, maybe what folks initially mean is that the preacher has said something profound. But I'd like to believe that heavy walkers and talkers are also grounded. They are weighed down by something supernatural.

The Black church calls it the anointing. That word, however, has become convoluted and distorted. In the advent of social media platforms and networks, "the anointing" as a phrase has been misinterpreted as charisma. But walking heavy is something else entirely. It's not personality. It's so much deeper. There is a groundedness to someone who is "talking heavy." They are rooted deeply.

Joy is also a grounding force. When you encounter someone filled with or operating in joy or someone who is moving in a joyous way, you might notice a heaviness to them. Not heavy as in dark or depressed. A heaviness more like in that old gospel song: steadfast and unmovable. Joy grounds us because it keeps us in touch with what matters. The deeper things. It helps us focus on the stuff that exists underneath the surface. Underneath the pain or trauma that has tried to take us out.

It's an interesting paradox, isn't it? We often talk about joy as an emotion that lifts, as in, "Her joy lifted our spirits." And it certainly does that universally. But when I think about Black joy, it's unique in that it lifts us, but it also grounds us. It holds us steady in the middle of the chaos.

I've always wanted our joy to be a much more expansive concept, and I think "joy as a grounding force" gets us there. Yes, we are lifted when we hear a song we love. We experience the high of pleasure when we are doing something that makes us happy. But consider all the ways maintaining our joy holds us steady when the proverbial boat is rocking.

In the same way a congregation calls back to a preacher, joy opens up dialogue at a spiritual level. If I can access my joy and joy gives me the words, I can talk back to that thing in my life, whatever it is. If something wonderful is happening, I can talk it through its birth.

And I get that we use birthing language for nearly everything nowadays, but I truly think that some of what we produce in our lives goes through a birthing process. There is gestation. A generative time. And then there's a time when we must push. We have to get that thing—book, business, better relationship—out of our imaginations and into the world. The language of joy lets us root ourselves as we pull that thing into fruition. It allows us to talk to that thing that's just beyond the horizon and say, "Come on now! You're walking heavy now! Here it comes. You got it."

EXERCISE YOUR JOY

Choose a project or venture that you want to "birth." Maybe it's a book, a new career or relationship, or even a personal goal. Walk through all the stages below and write in detail what you plan to do for each.

Generation

This is before the seed is selected. Brainstorm all the possible versions of your project.

_____

_____

_____

_____

_____

_____

_____

_____

_____

_____

_____

_____

Gestation

Okay, you know specifically what this thing is. You must nurture and feed it until it's ready to make its way into the world.

_____

_____

_____

_____

_____

_____

_____

_____

Delivery

Now it's time to release/launch/birth this thing into the world! What steps will you take to do it?

_____

_____

_____

_____

_____

_____

_____

_____

*May I always be weighed down
with the fullness of joy.*

Today I will choose joy by . . .

Handwriting a letter. To a friend. A family member. Myself.
Joy is the intention of this letter. To encourage and uplift. To share
a funny moment or a movie/album recommendation.

Or . . .

(Fill in the one thing you'll choose to do today to experience joy.)

_____

_____

_____

_____

_____

_____

_____

THE PLAY BY PLAY

Use this page to journal any additional thoughts or reflections that come to mind.

Day 21

THE VEHICLE
OF SOUL CARE

*You were not just born to center your entire existence
on work and labor. You were born to heal, to grow,
to be of service to yourself and community, to practice,
to experiment, to create, to have space,
to dream, and to connect.*

—TRICIA HERSEY,
Rest Is Resistance: A Manifesto

The first time my daughter got sick, I was a mess. She was barely two years old, and up until that point, we hadn't dealt with any issues besides a minor sniffle here or there with maybe a little sneeze or cough on occasion. But this was the flu, and her fever had hit 103. She cried throughout the night and was in so much pain.

Despite trying all the things—over-the-counter medicines, cool baths—we could not break her fever. I felt such a sense of helplessness because I couldn't stand to see her suffer. I didn't want to let nature take its course, as so many people suggested. In my mind, nature was taking entirely too long. But we had no choice. There was nothing more we could do except be a comfort to her. So that's what we did. I laid her next to me in the bed so I could monitor her fever. I simply kissed, hugged, and held her until this awful thing moved through her body.

After the fever broke and she started to feel better, I reflected on my response to her illness. It was second nature for me, as her mother, to do everything I possibly could to make her feel comfortable. There was never any doubt in my mind that I should do anything other than that. So why is it that when *I'm* not feeling well, when *my* body is hurting, when *my* heart and mind are all over the place with anxiety and I'm in need of deep care, I don't respond to *my own* need with that same kind of urgency? Why don't I take care of *myself* in the same ways I take care of my child and others I love?

The answer was hard for me to swallow, especially since it was wrapped in a bunch of stuff related to worth and self-esteem. See, with my daughter, I am adamant about teaching her all the things she needs to do for herself to be well. As parents, we tell our children to go to bed early because it's important for their health and mood to be rested, yet we stay up all night scrolling on social media. We tell them to eat their veggies and we feed them the best food we can within our means, yet we eat junk. Even beyond our children, we have more advice, more grace, and more discernment for others than we allow for ourselves. We are more than willing to encourage our friends to keep going in their job search or advise them to let go of that romantic relationship that isn't serving them well. Yet . . .

There is too often a disconnect between the way we care for others and the way we treat ourselves, and if we want to sit in the fullness of joy, we must address this.

Sometimes when we talk about joy, we think of our participation in events happening outside ourselves. And that's absolutely one iteration of joy. We can find it in serving our families. We can have joy in attending a celebration of someone we love. But we can also experience joy in self-care, in creating safety and calm and peace in our own bodies . . . for ourselves. Remember when I said joy can be a grounding force? Well, grounding happens in self-care. In soul care. Doing something we love, for no other reason except loving it, roots us in a sense of inherent worthiness.

Here's the beauty of it all: The more we take care of ourselves, the more we open up our capacity to experience more joy. Many of us can't experience joy because we are too tired. We are exhausted. We aren't eating right. We're not moving enough. We're not doing all the basic things for our bodies and minds that will then open up the opportunity for us to experience joy the way we would really like to.

And I'm not just talking about bubble baths and nail salon visits, although those are great forms of self-care for many people. I'm also thinking about our minds and souls. Soul care can potentially look like scheduling a few sessions with a therapist. Opening a sacred text. Getting a budget-friendly hotel room and doing a staycation where all you do is sleep and order food delivery. Rest is soul care.

So today let's consider how we are treating our bodies. Are we caring for them in the way we need to so that when joy comes up in us, we'll have the ability to grab on to it? I want to get to the point where I'm never too tired or busy to go to the beach. Never too wiped out to have a five-minute dance break with my child. Never too depleted to do the things I know will make me smile or laugh or feel good. Soul care provides an opportunity for joy to show up, and once we understand that connection, we'll see a difference in the way we prioritize our own well-being.

EXERCISE YOUR JOY

Fill in the chart below. After you finish, use the Play by Play section to reflect on what you wrote. What do you observe about how much you're pouring out to others and how much you're giving to yourself? Does it seem like you value productivity more than rest and wellness?

Ways I Care for Others	Ways I Care for Myself

May I always choose to take care of my soul.

Today I will choose joy by . . .

Drinking eight glasses or four sixteen-ounce bottles of water. Because I know that my body is made of almost two-thirds water and that drinking water sustains my physical self in a way that not much else does.

Or . . .

(Fill in the one thing you'll choose to do today to experience joy.)

_____

_____

_____

_____

_____

_____

_____

THE PLAY BY PLAY

Use this page to journal any additional thoughts or reflections that come to mind.

JOY IN THE LAUGHTER

Day 22

LAUGH, AND LAUGH SOME MORE

Determine to live life with flair and laughter.
—MAYA ANGELOU

I like to laugh. In recent years, as I've learned more about the power of laughter to heal our physical bodies, I've embraced my laughter even more. In fact, sometimes I intentionally seek out laughter. In those weeks when I was ill in 2019 (as I mentioned in the introduction), one of the things I did to help rightsize the grief, rage, and physical pain I was experiencing was binge-watch nearly every single stand-up comedy show that existed. I watched comedians I likely never would have watched prior to being stuck in bed all day. Every morning, I lined up the shows I wanted to watch in my queue and settled into a day of sometimes utter foolery.

I didn't really recognize this then, but in hindsight, watching those shows gave me a respite from my pain. It interrupted all the thoughts that were swirling in my mind about what was going on in my body. It distracted me from all the stories I'd made up about my pain and gave my mind, body, and spirit time to rest and allow joy to do its healing work.

When I was laughing, I wasn't thinking about the next doctor's appointment. I wasn't rehashing all the things I could have done in the past, all the better food I could have eaten, all the exercise I could have done. I wasn't doing any of that. I was still. Not silent—because, listen, I laugh loudly. I howl. I guffaw. Whatever you want to call it. But my mind and heart weren't racing. And that's the beauty and power of laughter. Though I might be laughing loudly, my heart and mind are still, and in that stillness, healing happens.

And it did. After months of tears all night and laughter all day, I got stronger. I jokingly call it my emotional purging. Eventually, I was able to set my cane aside and return to writing and teaching.

I encourage you to seek laughter too. Got a funny friend? Call them up. While you shouldn't want to *use* your friend, if you're close with the person, you can easily say, "Hey, friend, I could really use a little bit of your joy today. I'm having a tough time." If you find yourself on social media quite a bit, search hashtags for funny content. I'll never forget the day I stumbled upon a video montage of Black people laughing. Yep, that's it. It was nothing but clips of our spontaneous combustions of joy. Black people bursting into good, hearty cackles. No context given whatsoever. We don't know why they're laughing. And we don't have to know. All we need to understand is that there is joy being had and we can partake. It was truly the most satisfying and hilarious series of videos I'd ever seen.

So many of the media images of Black, Brown, and Indigenous people reflect our pain and trauma. But that is, by far, not the totality of who we are. Our dehumanization by systems, though very real and very much a point of protest, is not the centerpiece of who we are individually or collectively.

Maybe you're not into social media. Okay, that's cool. Do you have children? Nieces and nephews? Godchildren? Go hang out with them. Kids will sometimes say the most off thing, something so out of this world, that you won't be able to help bursting into laughter. If anything, you'll learn to be present. Laughter requires us to be present. And it's in that presence that joy is unearthed.

So, what's the point, Tracey? I watch a bunch of funny videos, hang out with kids, seek joy everywhere, and then what?

Joy is contagious, friend. I can almost guarantee that it will be nearly impossible to hold back your own laughter in the presence of such joy. And because some of us struggle with generating joy from our own insides, you can consider the joy you discover as a kind of fire starter, a way in which your own laughter becomes a salve for whatever you might be experiencing in the moment.

Some of us are so deep in the weeds when it comes to our trauma and pain that we will have to, at least in the beginning, actively seek out our joy. We might even have to manufacture scenarios and circumstances that are going to create it for us. Sure, it's great to have those organic, spontaneous moments when laughter just shows up; those are powerful. But sometimes we have to put ourselves in positions for joy to find us. Or for the joy that already exists deep down inside us to feel safe enough to show up.

EXERCISE YOUR JOY

Create an emergency laugh list. This will be a minimum of seven movies, songs, stories, books, TikTok videos—anything, really—that immediately make you laugh. Use this list as another resource on your joy journey.

1. _____

2. _____

3. _____

4. _____

5. _____

6. _____

7. _____

Today's Meditation

May I seek out laughter as much as I can,
for as long as I can.

Today I will choose joy by ...

Watching or listening to the very first entry on my emergency laugh list.
Who doesn't need to laugh immediately and always?

Or ...

(Fill in the one thing you'll choose to do today to experience joy.)

_____

_____

_____

_____

_____

_____

_____

_____

THE PLAY BY PLAY

Use this page to journal any additional thoughts or reflections that come to mind.

_____

_____

_____

_____

_____

_____

_____

_____

_____

_____

_____

_____

_____

_____

_____

_____

_____

_____

THE ANIMATION OF OUR JOY

The Black Church

The whooping cadence of the pastor.
The exuberant rejoicing of a choir.
The call-and-response of the congregation.
The rocking, moaning, or tongue-talking prayers.
The shouting and stomping and running in praise.
The testifying and baptizing.
The anointing oil and being slain in the spirit.
The post-service fried-chicken plates,
pound cake, and red punch.
The joy of fellowship and community.
The joy ... always the joy.

My experience growing up in the Black church is a complicated one, for sure. But if there is one thing I deeply treasure about it, it's the force of spirituality that shows up in that space. The sounds and voices and movement that define it are so integral to my understanding of God and divinity, and I would not trade that for the world. When a Black church is authentic and rooted in an understanding of God that's deeper than its proximity to Western Christianity, it is the most contemplative and sacred and holy place I know.

Contemplative theologian Barbara A. Holmes writes about this space quite a bit. When we think about church in general and contemplative/spiritual practices in particular, we too often only think of quiet. We think of silent meditation and liturgical worship. We assume that the Spirit truly shows up only in silence. We wrongly equate stillness and deep spirituality with that quiet and silence. Sadly, that is one of many subtle ways Eurocentrism has influenced the way we receive the concept of inner stillness and ultimately the church. And that's marginalizing at best. Especially when the Black church, culturally, tends to offer an animated, emotional experience, where there is boisterous preaching, singing, and shouting. We "get happy" and share our joy in vocal, yet absolutely sacred, ways.

In the middle of our "noise," a contemplative quality is still present. "Contemplation is not confined to designated and institutional sacred spaces," Holmes wrote. "Some sacred places bear none of the expected characteristics. The fact that we prefer stained glass windows, pomp and circumstance . . . has nothing to do with the sacred."[7] This is true. The Black church is a witness. It is also ground zero for Black joy and all the ways it is demonstrated.

Day 23

THE FUEL FOR IMAGINATION

Watch us walk, watch us move, watch us overcome, listen to our voices, the sway. The resilience. The innovation. The raw, unfiltered and untouched soul.

—SOLANGE KNOWLES

It was day five. I'd been sitting in front of my computer, trying to bring the words I knew were deep down inside me out and onto the page. But it was hard. So hard. I knew what I wanted to say. I knew what I *needed* to say. I have such a love for you, reader-friend, and for the people I know are on the other end of this process, that I desperately wanted to make sure what I was offering was worthy of attention.

I often resist the phrase "writer's block" because oftentimes I think what we mean by writer's block is likely something much deeper. Nothing is truly blocking us from writing unless someone has smashed our computer to pieces and thrown out our pen and paper. And on that day, the only thing that was truly blocking me from writing was . . . well, me.

So, what *is* writer's block (or artist's, dancer's, student's, lawyer's, or doctor's block)? I like to think of it as a resistance to letting go. The thing that blocks me from putting down the words in my head and heart is my inability to free myself from whatever stories I've been telling about myself or the work. When we hold on too tightly to something—a thought, even—then the act of holding on becomes a roadblock for our creativity, innovation, or expression of ideas. We are in our own way. And on that day, I was certainly in my own way.

Anyone embarking on a task, especially a creative one, needs to have a certain amount of imagination to show up and do the thing that one feels called to do. And as I sat at the computer and stared at my cursor blinking on a blank Word document, I realized that my inability to call for the imagination I needed was very much related to my inability to connect to my joy. For me, a struggle to access joy is a clear indication that I will struggle in the writing process. When I allow myself the space to experience joy, essentially I am telling my body and mind to release their hold on anything negative; I can be free. That freedom then inevitably carries over into my creative work.

The way we can navigate the resistance that shows up when we have to be creative is by choosing to give ourselves a moment of reprieve. Pleasure is powerful. The act of embracing joy and pleasure, if we do it consistently, allows us to make room for innovation.

Remember when I said joy expands us? It doesn't take away our pain or grief, but it does make us bigger. It allows us to have more room for things like creativity. So when we are calling upon our imaginations to create a thing—whatever that thing is—we can trust that joy has made room for it. If we have been in the practice of making joy an ever-present undercurrent in our lives, it is a lot easier to tap into our imaginations.

I encourage you today to really think about when you have been stuck. Maybe you're trying to solve a problem on the job or write the next great film and something doesn't feel quite right. Take a minute and go do something that brings you joy. Find something that will give you a brief moment of pleasure. Use joy to unlock more space in your mind and spirit and tell your body, *It's okay to be free and release.*

On day five of being unable to write, I decided to take a walk instead of trying to plow through the chapters I needed to write. I walked through our neighborhood, with all its beautiful trees and the calming sounds of nature. I stopped at the playground to swing because there's something special and rejuvenating about touching the sky. Then I returned to my desk and the same Word document with its same flashing curser. If I'm honest, there were no floodgates thrown wide by my short walk. It was more like a window had been slightly cracked. But it was enough. My imagination had an opening. And I finished the—this—chapter.

EXERCISE YOUR JOY

Name your blocks. Maybe you don't have a writing block, but you might be experiencing other things that are blocking your access to joy. Name them in the squares here and on the next page, and then attach an action of joy to each. Make a commitment to enact your joy whenever you are faced with that block in particular.

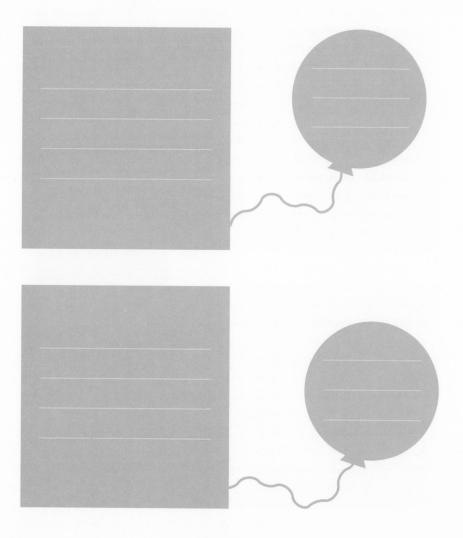

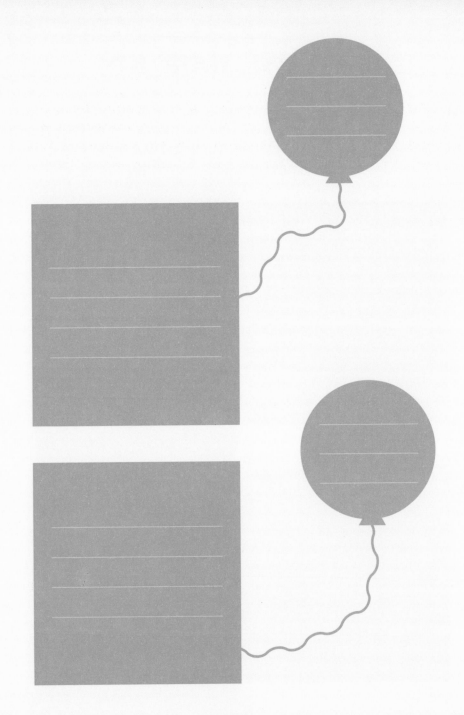

May I allow joy to drive my creativity.

Today I will choose joy by . . .

Playing a video game. Or a game I love on my phone.
Maybe it's Scrabble or Wordle. Maybe it's Fortnite or NBA 2K.
Maybe it's an intense session of Candy Crush.

Or . . .

(Fill in the one thing you'll choose to do today to experience joy.)

_____

_____

_____

_____

_____

_____

_____

THE PLAY BY PLAY

Use this page to journal any additional thoughts or reflections that come to mind.

Day 24

REGULAR, DEGULAR JOY

Impossibilities are merely things of which we have not learned. or which we do not wish to happen.

—CHARLES W. CHESNUTT,
The Complete Works of Charles W. Chesnutt

I was never a liar. At least not intentionally so. As a child, I was more into the art of exaggeration. I would extend the truth beyond the bounds of normality, making things more fantastic than I believed the reality to be. So, yes, my pain was always bigger than maybe it actually was, but so was my joy.

Oh well, Tracey. That's just what kids do. They exaggerate.

Yes, they do. Yet I'm beginning to see how it was more than that.

When I was a child, part of me often felt like the truth as it was, or my story as it was, was not quite enough. So I felt compelled to tailor my story to the audience. If I was sharing something with my parents that happened at school that day and I knew they wanted to see me in a particular light, I would skew that very real, very true story so they would see me in that light. If I was talking with my friends at school on Monday morning about something that happened on the weekend and wanted them to believe me to be cool, I would make the story of that very real, fun thing as cool as I possibly could to grab their attention. At its core, this wasn't a good thing to do, for sure. But I do think the ability to use my imagination to find any nugget of joy amid what I viewed as ordinary has now become useful as I navigate days where I'm hard-pressed to find any good.

I suppose there are two parts of this, then. First, there's the need for all of us to accept regular, degular (thanks, Cardi B) joy. And to not feel as though we have to make our "good things" bigger and better than they are. Yes, we can have an amazing joy moment on that grand girls' trip to Mexico with gloriously wonderful things happening every day, and we can also have an amazing, equally worth-sharing joy moment by taking a thirty-minute catnap in the middle of the day.

The joy born from grand events is great but not always sustainable. If we are relying on only the big joys to fill us, we may find ourselves wanting. But if we're trying to write in our joy on our daily to-do lists, it's important to consider what are seemingly the small joys. What are the things that give you joy but aren't necessarily activities of grandeur? Maybe it is just taking a walk when you need it. And maybe that walk doesn't have to be made into some deep, revelatory experience where you meditate on the birds that circle the trees. Maybe you can just take a walk to move your body. That's 100 percent okay.

Second, you can find value in seeing your circumstances through the lens of joy in a way that may not appear obvious at first. If I'm going through a hard time because I'm trying to meet a deadline for a book and my focus is off or I am struggling to find the right words, I can create a scenario in my mind that helps me accomplish that goal. I can see the project I'm working on as bigger than it is in order to create some motivation. I can say, *This book is going to bless the world!*, and maybe that's true or maybe it isn't, but if the joy that thought generates for me will actually help me push through, then it's worth it.

At the end of the day, regular Black joy matters. The passing of laws and policies that support racial justice matters. The decision to take our Black families on regular vacations to make rest a priority also matters. It's both/and, never either/or. And instead of having a tendency to exaggerate in order to stretch the truth like little Tracey did, we can use it to fuel our imaginations and get us to the joy moment we've been looking for.

EXERCISE YOUR JOY

Find a little unexpected joy today. Log in to any music-streaming app (Spotify, Apple, Amazon) and search for songs that have the word *joy* in the title. Take some time to listen to music you may have never heard before or haven't heard in a long time. Then create a joy playlist of ten new favorites.

1. _____

2. _____

3. _____

4. _____

5. _____

6. _____

7. _____

8. _____

9. _____

10. _____

*May I know that all forms of joy, big or small,
are healing.*

Today I will choose joy by . . .

Smiling at a minimum of three people. For no reason. Even if I don't feel like it.
Because I know that a simple joy like smiling goes a long way.

Or . . .

(Fill in the one thing you'll choose to do today to experience joy.)

_____

_____

_____

_____

_____

_____

_____

_____

THE PLAY BY PLAY

Use this page to journal any additional thoughts or reflections that come to mind.

_____

_____

_____

_____

_____

_____

_____

_____

_____

_____

_____

_____

_____

_____

_____

_____

Day 25

JOY IN COMMUNITY

Rarely, if ever, are any of us healed in isolation. Healing is an act of communion.

—BELL HOOKS, *All About Love*

I could not wait to get to my girlfriend's house. I had my big church-lady hat on and was wearing my fancy gloves. Four friends and I were gathering to celebrate one another and wanted to do something different as a theme, so we decided on a tea party! Four good and grown Black women at that! I was totally there for it. In addition to good food (and, of course, tea of all kinds), we had a ball playing games and talking about everything under the sun. The conversation wound effortlessly through our church, relationships, and children. But most of all, we just offered what I like to call "silent support."

When sister-friends gather, oftentimes there are the things we are talking and laughing about and then there are the things that go unsaid. If we are close, we already know one another's stories. We've already had those crying or cussing moments as a group when life starts life-ing. But when we are enjoying being together and having fun, we don't always want to dig that stuff up. We want to laugh and feel the love and freedom that come with relationship. And the beauty of that kind of joy is that it allows for the unsaid stuff to actually be supported in those moments. The more we enjoy one another's company, the more we provide a place for all those things we aren't saying to just be.

At our tea party, the ladies and I played a game called Heads Up! It's a phone app that's very similar to charades or Taboo. A word pops up on the screen, and a player must put the phone on their forehead so they can't see the word but the rest of the people in the room can. Their team then will describe the word to the player while being timed and without using any part of the word. Listen when I tell you this game sent us to heaven (or hell, depending on the word) so many times. We screamed and laughed and acted out the words like we were Angela Bassett or Viola Davis. Our joy was palpable.

But what I most remember besides all the laughter was the fact that this game brought all our various experiences together in a way where we all fit. Some of us are Gen X, while others are millennials. Some of us have no children, while others of us have multiples. Some of us are stay-at-home moms, and others work full-time. The game made it so none of that mattered and all of it mattered. It leveled the playing field so that either we knew the movie *The Breakfast Club* or we didn't, and either way, it was okay. (I knew it, by the way. Gen X forever.)

The time spent with those women really showed me the importance of having a joyful community that can support you and with whom you can share your joy moments. Having a sisterhood or brotherhood or village where love is the common denominator and joy is the expression is beautiful. It becomes a landing place for the said and unsaid. A space where everyone strives to provide not just advice or a shoulder for tears but a place for gut-level laughter that makes your stomach hurt so good.

Friends are great for instigating joy. I encourage us to prioritize our healthy platonic relationships in the same ways we do our romantic ones. Then we'll inevitably see more joy in our lives.

EXERCISE YOUR JOY

Answer this question in the Play by Play section: What do you require in a friend? Reciprocation? Empathy? A heavy-handed wine pour?

Sometimes we think we know what we want in our close platonic relationships, but, in truth, we haven't really thought about it. We've simply become friends because of proximity and shared interests. That is fine, of course, but as we become more intentional on this joy journey, it will become increasingly important to evaluate what we want in our friendships. And then proceed accordingly.

May I maintain or build a joyful village of support.

Today I will choose joy by . . .

Sending a funny or encouraging message to my friend group.
Because I know that sometimes a little light can reclaim a dark day.

Or . . .

(Fill in the one thing you'll choose to do today to experience joy.)

_____

_____

_____

_____

_____

_____

_____

_____

THE PLAY BY PLAY

Use this page to journal any additional thoughts or reflections that come to mind.

_____

_____

_____

_____

_____

_____

_____

_____

_____

_____

_____

_____

_____

_____

_____

_____

_____

_____

_____

JOY IN THE EVERY DAY

Day 26

IN SERVICE TO OURSELVES

Miracles happen all the time.
We're here, aren't we?

—MARILYN NELSON, "Abba Jacob and Miracles"

I was taught that service means the most in life. It didn't matter whether it was church or some special auxiliary organization I was part of as a child. Service was king. Even in school, I was taught to live by a quote that's often attributed to Muhammad Ali: "Service to others is the rent you pay for your room here on earth."

I do think there is truth in this. Service is incredibly important. More than any singular act, service is a posture of one's heart. It's an inclination to care for others. But I also think that sometimes some of us become defined by it.

Those of us who grew up in the Black church might remember that one elder who was the head of the usher board and took her job *way* too seriously. I imagine that if she were told that she could no longer be an usher, she might feel as though she'd lost her purpose. She might feel useless even though God could and likely would lead her into other ways of serving. But because being an usher was her entire personality and she gave her whole self over to the role, she might feel unsettled without that title. This is a prime example of a person who has defined herself by her service to her own detriment.

When we allow ourselves to be solely defined by our service, we can forget to serve ourselves. We can forget to show ourselves as much compassion as we show others. This can show up in a myriad of ways. The mom who throws elaborate birthday parties for her children but doesn't celebrate her own day. The executive who works late and goes above and beyond but never takes a vacation. The performer who does "one more show" despite being sick and exhausted.

I think that is often why many people who work in service fields start off as kind, generous individuals who truly enjoy what they do but ultimately end up as rude and short somewhere along the line. They become burned-out because they've poured out so much to others but have never taken the time to fill themselves up.

It's so important that we don't do the healing work of reclaiming our joy (especially when that joy is associated with our work) only to give so much of ourselves that we lose the joy we found in serving in the first place. This just sets us up to turn in on ourselves. A lack of self-compassion looks like not resting, not taking breaks, and not making room for play, all of which result in a lack of the compassion we need to love and serve others the way we desire to.

What I've come to learn over time is that the more compassion we have for ourselves, the more compassion we can offer to others. The more we keep our cups full, the more we have to pour out. The more joy we allow ourselves to experience, the more joy we're able to allow other people around us to experience. Showing ourselves kindness makes room for us to freely show kindness to other people. We can't authentically give what we haven't first practiced in our own bodies and spirits.

EXERCISE YOUR JOY

As we're thinking about creating these joy moments, a really great starting point can be looking at what we're already doing in service to others and asking ourselves whether there is some way we can turn that service toward ourselves. How can we give to ourselves in the same ways we give to others?

I had a friend once say to me, "Tracey, you give great advice, but you're not really all that great at taking your own advice." It was absolutely true, although it was another one of those truths I hated to hear. But I knew she was saying it out of love. She went on to suggest that I should treat myself like I would treat a friend who was coming to me with the same issues I had. What would I tell a person who is tired all the time? Well, nine times out of ten, I would tell them to incorporate naps into their day. Or to go to bed an hour earlier. She encouraged me to treat myself like I'm the bestie who needs a good talking-to. It was such a great idea, and it really got me thinking about why I struggled with loving myself the same way I love others.

If you're reading this and journaling something like, *I'm still wrestling with figuring out what gives me joy,* then maybe do a little role-play with yourself. Pretend that same statement is being said to you by a friend and you have taken them aside to offer some guidance. What would you say? Would you ask when the last time was that they smiled? Or had a deep-in-the-gut laugh? When they felt settled and at peace in their body and heart? What gets them excited? Ask them (which, of course, is actually you) and see what happens.

Issues I struggle with	Advice I would give

Today's Meditation

May I serve myself just as well as I serve others.

Today I will choose joy by . . .

Drinking my favorite beverage. And savoring it. No scrolling my phone while drinking it. No doing homework. Simply sitting and drinking, drinking and sitting. Yes, sometimes it's that simple.

Or . . .

(Fill in the one thing you'll choose to do today to experience joy.)

_____

_____

_____

_____

_____

_____

_____

_____

THE PLAY BY PLAY

Use this page to journal any additional thoughts or reflections that come to mind.

Day 27

LEAPS OF FAITH

Give light, and people will find a way.
—ELLA BAKER

When I graduated from college in 1996, the quiet desire I had to write professionally was overshadowed by what I had always been taught I *should* want. I was supposed to want a good job, making good money, with good benefits. Yes, I deeply wanted to share stories of healing and triumph and joy with the world, but I wasn't quite sure how to do that and still eat. Plus, I was wrestling with all the ways I felt inadequate and unworthy of telling those stories.

I told myself that my passion would have to wait, and I jumped into a career path that I excelled in but that offered no fulfillment. For six years, I worked in sales and marketing for a couple of Fortune 500 companies until I couldn't take the feeling of restlessness anymore. I wasn't listening to my life. I wasn't listening to God's guidance and direction *for* my life. And as a result, there was always a dark cloud hovering over my successes in that field.

Bottom line? There was no joy.

I didn't like uncertainty. I was always scared of the unknown. But an old saying I'd heard before rang true for me in that season: Change happens when the pain of remaining the same becomes greater than the pain of taking a leap of faith. Or as Granny used to say, "It doesn't bother you enough yet." That was it.

It was becoming too emotionally and spiritually painful to not do what I felt called to do. I wasn't good at going numb like some people I knew. They were able to compartmentalize their pain. They were able to push down those feelings of wanting to do something else and keep their noses to the grindstone. I could not. I felt everything. And while it was certainly a risk to leave my well-paying job to focus on writing—a career path that, in the beginning, paid a grand old salary of $0.00—I didn't want to not try. It was hard. One of the hardest things I'd ever done up until that point. There were adjustments to be made. But I'd done hard things before. I'd adjusted before. I just needed to trust that God would work it out in my favor.

The pursuit of joy you are undertaking may require a leap of faith. It will likely require you to do things you've never done before and be willing to be vulnerable in ways that you might not be used to. Sometimes even when we decide to trust God instead of our own minds about this thing we're embarking upon, we don't always experience a smooth transition.

Stepping out of my comfort zone was very tough for me. I know from personal experience that even once you take the leap, it can be really easy to veer off course. The adversaries in our lives will convince us that we have done the wrong thing or that we have no purpose. There might even be traumatized parts of ourselves that tell us that this decision we've made isn't safe, based upon long-past experiences those parts want us to keep responding to.

For me, this looked like jumping right back into full-time positions—this time in fields such as museum curation, small-business development, and academia—only five years after making the decision to pursue writing. Listen, I was confused. I wanted to write, to tell my stories. But I wanted the safety those other fields offered. And I didn't yet know whether God would make both happen.

Nonetheless, even amid that uncertainty, I remained grounded in the understanding that the vision I had for my life was bigger than where I was or whatever choice I made in any given moment. I could see the joy I was missing out on and knew that the only way I'd be able to access it was if I always followed my heart and let God order my steps.

The same goes for you, friend. As your healing is in process, your destiny is in progress, and joy is the pathway.

EXERCISE YOUR JOY

Write a joy script using the prompts below. The script will be the words you will say to yourself whenever uncertainty, grief, rage, or any other emotion feels overwhelming. Acknowledging the truth of what you're feeling is important. But so is managing your self-talk so that you are speaking life to yourself.

I am feeling uncertain, and I also

_____

_____

I am feeling angry, and I also

_____

_____

I am feeling sad, and I also

_____

_____

I am feeling _____, and I also

_____

_____

_____

_____

_____

Today's Meditation

May I find peace with uncertainty as well as trust the joy to come.

Today I will choose joy by . . .

Trying something new. Stepping out of a comfort zone or rut might mean doing something unfamiliar and breaking up old patterns. So, if I usually go straight home from work, why not meet up with a friend for dinner? Do I normally bring a turkey sandwich for lunch? Why not try tuna?

Or . . .

(Fill in the one thing you'll choose to do today to experience joy.)

_____

_____

_____

_____

_____

_____

_____

_____

THE PLAY BY PLAY

Use this page to journal any additional thoughts or reflections that come to mind.

_____

_____

_____

_____

_____

_____

_____

_____

_____

_____

_____

_____

_____

_____

_____

_____

_____

_____

Day 28

SURRENDER THE OUTCOMES

So don't worry about tomorrow, for tomorrow will bring its own worries. Today's trouble is enough for today.

—MATTHEW 6:34, NLT

Recently, my daughter and I have been butting heads somewhat, as often happens when a child is transitioning into the tween and teen years. I know she is trying to find her way. Even while wanting to be a child, cuddling with Mommy before bed, and feeling all the safety that comes with being a little kid, she is also wanting more independence and freedom to define herself above and beyond the ideals Mom and Dad might have for her.

The struggle can be so challenging at times. Often, I have to sit with myself and realize how agitated I am because things aren't going the way I thought they would. I want things to be right, but I also realize I have a very narrow view of what "right" looks like. It's not so much that things are going horribly; it's more that I can't anticipate the outcome and, in terms of how I view myself as a parent, have had to shift and change more than I would like.

The truth is, my daughter and I are learning from each other. We are navigating this experience together as opposed to my solely guiding and leading her. I think that's okay. But, of course, there's part of my body that has only the way I was raised—with a very top-down power dynamic—as a point of reference. So sometimes what I know in my heart is okay still feels wrong. Thank God I know that feelings are not facts.

Whenever we are trying to do a new thing, something unfamiliar like, oh, say, implementing more joy in our lives, we are bound to have some discomfort. It takes time for those parts of ourselves to adjust to this new way of being and doing. That's why it's important to have a good support system, to have people who have earned the right to hear your story, as sociologist Brené Brown would say.[8] People we trust. Because inevitably when we share how we are feeling, we may find out we're not alone. That's the power of community. It can quell the shaking of our hearts and the anxiety in our minds, especially when it comes to parenting.

Recently, I shared some of my mom challenges with a social media forum for mothers with tween girls. I explained how I thought I was screwing up badly. How I didn't think I had the capacity to give the guidance my daughter needed. The response was simply overwhelming.

"Oh, girl, you are not alone!"

"I've been there. Can't say it gets easier, but it's always worth it."

"Keep trying. God knew who to send her to."

One of the biggest lessons I gleaned from those conversations with other moms was that as parents, we can absolutely set the conditions for our children but we must surrender the outcomes. In other words, we can create an environment that's loving and empathetic but also has boundaries and clear guidance and discipline. We can provide a space where our children feel safe enough to come talk to us. We *don't* get to control how they utilize what we've provided as they grow up. We *don't* get to control the outcomes. In fact, all we can do is trust that God is in it and believe that whatever we think we are missing will show up in some other kind of way as our kids need it.

When I consider all the ways I've tried to help my daughter access joy in her own life—joy that's not connected to what her friends think or dependent upon whether or not she gets a like on her TikTok dance video—I realize I must accept that whether or not she makes room for joy in her life is up to her. She actually has to do the work. She has her own joy journey to make. My job is simply to teach and model a version of a joyful life to her. To demonstrate how to hold both joy and pain simultaneously by how I approach my own life. But I don't necessarily get to determine what joy looks like for her and how she should wield it in her own life. And that's the hardest thing for all of us parents, isn't it?

We can build our playbook and create our arsenal of tools and resources that allow us to be able to give ourselves permission to experience joy and amplify it to those around us. We can go through the healing process that comes when we embark on our joy journeys. But we don't get to decide who accepts the path we are on. Just because we are intentional about bringing joy to all the spaces we're in doesn't mean that everybody's going to receive that joy well or at all. In truth, sometimes our joy may shine a light on the lack of joy in another person's life. And if that person is not at a place where they can accept that realization, they may react negatively to our happiness.

To be clear, joy is undeniably contagious. We should *want* to continue to be light everywhere we go. We just don't get to control how people receive our joy. But shine anyway, friend. Shine anyway.

EXERCISE YOUR JOY

Journal your answers to the following questions.

What are two areas of my life where I have unreasonable expectations or am overly invested in a particular outcome?

_____

_____

_____

_____

_____

_____

How can I approach these areas differently as I surrender the outcomes to God?

_____

_____

_____

_____

_____

_____

_____

May I do what I can do and allow myself
to be surprised by the end result.

Today I will choose joy by . . .

Not planning my day. Just for today, I will not look at my to-do
list if possible. I will let the day take me wherever it wants.
I will follow my bliss.

Or . . .

(Fill in the one thing you'll choose to do today to experience joy.)

_____

_____

_____

_____

_____

_____

_____

THE PLAY BY PLAY

Use this page to journal any additional thoughts or reflections that come to mind.

_____

_____

_____

_____

_____

_____

_____

_____

_____

_____

_____

_____

_____

_____

_____

_____

_____

_____

THE ANIMATION OF OUR JOY

The Beauty Salon and Barbershop

"You have a few more minutes under the dryer. You ain't dry yet, girl." (Insert Michael Jordan crying meme here.)

Historically, the beauty salon and barbershop in the Black community have been both hubs of information and centers of joy. In the same way the Black church once felt like a sacred ground zero for our demonstrations of joy, these spaces were also havens of pleasure. Places where we could see and be seen. When we entered those buildings, kitchens, and basements, we hoped to leave feeling and looking better than we did when we entered. It didn't matter if we were getting a press and curl, a relaxer, or a twist out on natural hair, whether we chose a Caesar cut or a fade, there is just something about the pending transformation of our appearance that fuels how we interact in that space. It's glorious!

As I was growing up, my mom was more of a kitchen-table beautician. I rarely went to the salon, and a family friend was who relaxed my hair for the first time. So when I got my first job at Kroger grocery, and later Burger King, I couldn't wait to have my own money so I could go on my own. In the salon, I found people from all different generations. I also discovered stacks of Black-owned publications like *Jet*, *Ebony*, and *Essence* magazines, or *Right On!* for us young uns. In those pages, I saw women who looked like me and women I hoped to look like one day.

Someone was always coming into the shop and selling something. The salon and barbershop screamed disposable income to those who were hustling to put food on the table, which wasn't entirely true. Yet we supported these local business owners the best we could. It didn't often matter if you believed in the product or whether you'd actually use those prepaid legal services or drink that noni juice; it was about seeing the face of that young brother or sister light up when you said you'd buy two fish plates or the CD mix or that Kush incense. It was about the idea that we had a space that felt safe for us to talk and be in ways that were more authentic than what we could ever do outside it.

If a song everyone loved came on the radio, folks could just sing aloud without being told to "bring it down."

And if everybody knew the lyrics to that Anita Baker or Luther Vandross or TLC song? Oh, then we were about to have a whole choir rehearsal in that place. At the end of the day, for Black folks, the salon or barbershop felt like joy because we were free there. It was home base for us. We were safe.

Day 29

DO YOU WANT TO BE WELL?

God gives nothing to those who keep their arms crossed.
—AFRICAN PROVERB

Sometimes asking a "silly question" isn't so silly after all. Let's consider John 5, verse 6. Jesus asked what seemed like a silly question to a man who had been lying beside a healing pool at Bethesda for thirty-eight years.

"Do you want to be well?"

I mean . . . yeah.

This question, on its surface, seems ridiculous, almost cruel even. To say this to a person who was in the right place and space to potentially be healed from what was making him sick but unable to make it happen? Yet a deeper dive into that question makes me think Jesus was onto something. It makes me wonder about all those moments when I was in the right place and space, had been in those spaces forever, but for some reason or another had not been able to access joy and, ultimately, healing. We've all been there, right?

You are almost finished with this journal. You have done the exercises and have written your heart out on these pages. You've sat in contemplation and figured out what joy feels like in your body.

You might even have a running joy list that you've written and put on your refrigerator or desk.

And it's entirely possible you still aren't sure what to do with it all. You are still struggling to access joy, even with all the guidance, affirmation, and information in the world.

When we find ourselves in the vicinity of wellness but languishing, it makes us ask, *Is healing really what we want? Is joy really what I want? Or am I just comfortable with my pain, the familiarity of my trauma?*

As I've said, this joy journey is a process. There is no destination, and, truthfully, it takes as long as it takes. That said, I do think it's important for you to reflect on why you might not have experienced as much progress as you would have liked. Are your expectations too high? Are you rushing the process? Okay, then stop that. But if you're not rushing, is it that you aren't as committed to accessing, creating, and amplifying joy as you should be? Are you just going through the motions because *Black joy* is the buzzword of the decade? Is there still a gap between what you say you want and what you're willing to work to get?

Now that we are near the end of this journey, ask yourself, *Do I want to be well? Do I truly desire joy?* What if wellness sits on the other side of grief? What if the only way forward is *through*? Are you willing to go *through* to get to your joy, to unearth it? Because, friend, it's there. It's always there. It's just waiting for you to stop ignoring all the things preventing you from seeing and feeling it.

EXERCISE YOUR JOY

Choose something from the joy list you began at the beginning of this journey. After you complete the activity, return to this page and spend some time drawing whatever comes to mind. You can doodle, draw a series of hash marks, or sketch a detailed self-portrait. The only rule is that I don't want you to think about what you're drawing. Just allow yourself the freedom to trust what comes.

In the Play by Play section, reflect on the influence your joy moment had on your creativity.

May I remember that I have a say
in being well and having joy.

Today I will choose joy by . . .

Practicing gratitude. I will make a list of ten things I'm grateful for in this
moment. I will then post that list somewhere I can see it daily.

1. _____   6. _____

2. _____   7. _____

3. _____   8. _____

4. _____   9. _____

5. _____   10. _____

Or . . .

(Fill in the one thing you'll choose to do today to experience joy.)

_____

_____

_____

THE PLAY BY PLAY

Use this page to journal any additional thoughts or reflections that come to mind.

_____

_____

_____

_____

_____

_____

_____

_____

_____

_____

_____

_____

_____

_____

_____

_____

_____

_____

_____

Day 30

A RECIPE FOR HEALING

For there is always light.
If only we're brave enough to see it.
If only we're brave enough to be it.

—AMANDA GORMAN,
"The Hill We Climb"

one part stillness
one part scream

both will help unravel your soul from the pain.

one part story
mixed with two parts surrender

these will ground you even as you fly.

a meditation, to taste.
a garden of plants that feed your body and heart.
the happy face of a fierce and fearless
eleven-year-old Brown baby girl.

these will offer your spirit a place to land.
a rhythm to dance to.
a ritual of reaping.

finally, a double dab of spice
laced in language.

because boundaries are a thing
and you've always been good at tests.

be sure that once your healing is mostly done
(because it never cooks all the way),
once it's cooled,
you sop up all the grace

with joy.

EXERCISE YOUR JOY

You did it, friend! You've just finished the first thirty days of your lifelong joy journey. You should absolutely be proud of yourself, because I know *I* am.

Yes, I know there might have been good days and not-so-good days. Days you journaled for an hour, and days when you could barely get three words down. It's okay! I firmly believe that every joy journey must be unique to the person on it. And our collective uniqueness is what can change the world.

For this final exercise, spend some time reflecting on the past thirty days. Any new revelations on what joy looks like for you? How will you proceed? Reflect in the Play by Play.

May I choose joy always.

(Fill in one more thing you'll choose to do today to experience joy.)

_____

_____

_____

_____

_____

_____

_____

THE PLAY BY PLAY

Use this page to journal any additional thoughts or reflections that come to mind.

_____

_____

_____

_____

_____

_____

_____

_____

_____

_____

_____

_____

_____

_____

_____

_____

_____